W9-BUQ-788

Our American Century

Pride and Prosperity · The 80s

★

By the Editors of Time-Life Books, Alexandria, Virginia

With a Foreword by Jesse Jackson

Contents

★

Foreword

During the 1980s I made a strong run for the Democratic presidential nomination, seeking an opportunity to do something for America's working people and the dispossessed. I felt that our nation had taken a wrong turn—away from the gains of the civil rights movement and toward unbridled greed and selfishness.

The nation chose for its leader Ronald Reagan, who rode into the White House promising smaller government, lower taxes, and less federal intrusion in people's lives. During this decade the stage was set for democracy's victory in the Cold War. And I also saw my friend Nelson Mandela of South Africa emerge from prison to begin leading one of the world's most amazing peaceful transformations from racist oppression and exclusion to democratic freedom.

Yet for all this progress the Reagan years saddled our country with grave problems. The government ran up the largest deficit in our history. Working people suffered as the value of their wages declined, their collective-bargaining powers withered, and public education deteriorated.

American culture changed radically during the decade. Hip-hop became a national craze, especially for African American youth looking for a way to be heard. Parents everywhere—black, white, and others—were mystified by the rhythms and appalled by some of the lyrics. Television also changed, as the dominance of the three broadcast networks was successfully challenged by cable TV. Bill Cosby, through his top-rated sitcom, gave white Americans a look at middle-class African American life. Oprah Winfrey helped to change the lives of millions of American women when she first began airing her show nationally.

What did the '80s teach us? That our future does not lie along the path of greed. That spirituality must enlighten our daily lives. That coming together remains the best way to achieve healthy and productive lives for all of us.

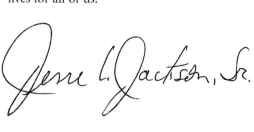

Spewing volcanic smoke and ash 60,000 feet skyward, Washington State's Mount St. Helens erupts on May 18, 1980, producing the most spectacular natural disaster of the decade.

The lovable star of E.T.: The Extra-Terrestrial bids a fond farewell to his earthling companion, played by 10-year-old Henry Thomas. By decade's end the film had reeled in more than $1 billion at the box office and another $400 million in video sales.

The personification of sporting grace and power, track star Jackie Joyner-Kersee tenses to hurl the javelin as part of a record-breaking 7,291-point heptathlon performance that earned her one of two gold medals at the 1988 Olympic Games.

Flags, photos, and mementos bear mute witness to the grief and loss represented by the stark black granite wall of the Vietnam Veterans Memorial in Washington, D.C. Dedicated in 1982, the monument lists 57,939 Americans killed in the war.

Diana, the new Princess of Wales, cheers up an overwrought young attendant—a five-year-old great-granddaughter of Winston Churchill whom she once taught in kindergarten—after her fairy-tale wedding to Prince Charles on July 29, 1981.

Shielded only by a sheet of plastic, a homeless man tries to keep warm on a snowy park bench near the White House. By the end of the decade, the problem of homelessness was growing and 30 million Americans were living below the poverty line.

Flaunting a Marilyn Monroe look, the ever out-rageous Madonna is caught in an act of ego-worship. The singer showed herself to be a master of self-promotion whose records, videos, and concerts earned her millions throughout the decade.

Saturn and its rings are captured up close and personal by NASA's 1981 Voyager 2 probe. Computer-generated colors in this composite photo reveal that the planet's surface is swept by wind belts whipping around at more than 1,000 miles an hour.

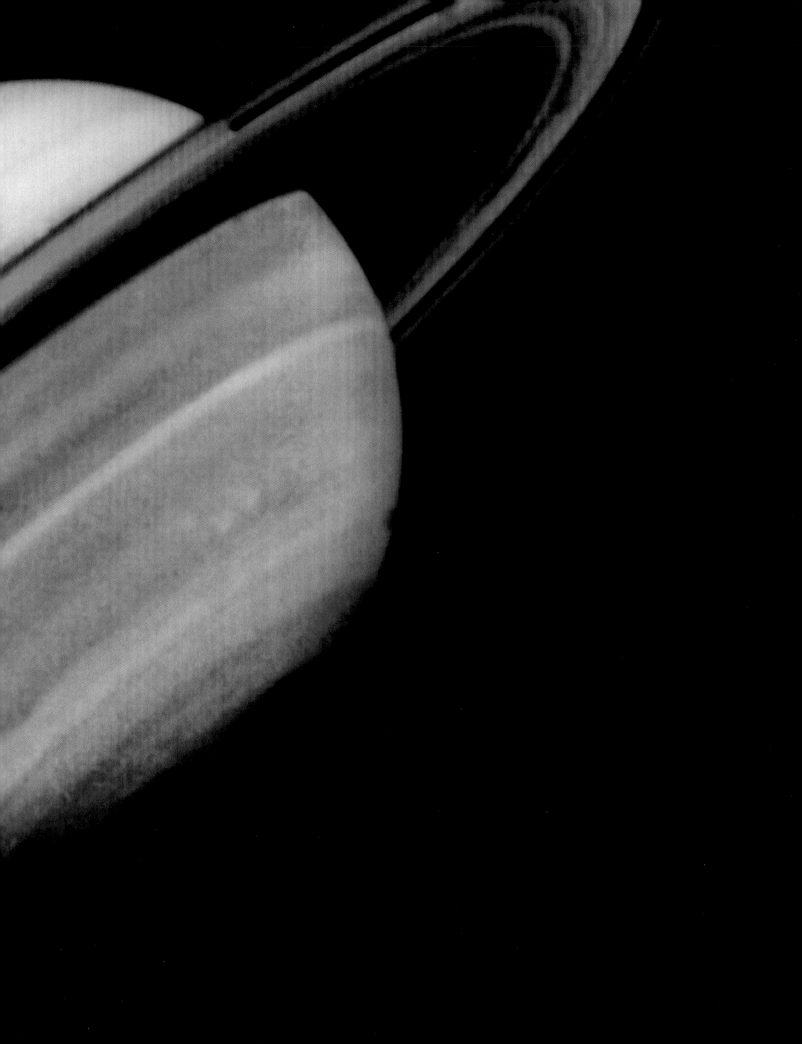

The Comeback Decade: 1980-1989

Here was the oldest man—he was in his 70s—ever to serve as president. Yet the boyish grin and rugged good looks still projected the youthful vigor of his days in Hollywood. When he spoke, there was the mellifluous voice and the familiar quick bob of the head. Then he would whip off a perfect 15-second sound bite for the network news or spin some tale with a moral.

It was the defining genius of Ronald Reagan to find parables of hope and optimism to sustain his vision of a reborn America. His predecessor, Jimmy Carter, had spoken of limits and the need for sacrifice. But Reagan utterly rejected that idea. After two decades of troubles—assassinations, urban riots, the agony of Vietnam, the disgrace of Watergate, energy crises, and double-digit inflation—the nation was ready for Reagan's exhortation to "dream heroic dreams." His feel-good conservatism embodied the 1980s—the restoration of pride and prosperity, but with little concern for pressing social and economic problems.

Reagan's appealing surface simplicity concealed a multitude of contradictions. He championed a return to family values, though he was the first divorced president in U.S. history and was estranged from several of his children. He cultivated fundamentalist Christians of the new religious right, calling for "a spiritual revival, a return to a belief in moral absolutes," but seldom attended church. He preached old-fashioned habits of work and productivity while maintaining a relaxed, hands-off management style and getting more sleep, it was said, than any president since Calvin Coolidge.

Good luck, as well as charisma, helped sustain Reagan's popularity. On the very day of his first inauguration came news of the release of the American hostages in Iran. Oil, the cause of so many of Carter's problems, flowed anew from the Middle East in relatively inexpensive abundance. He survived when would-be assassin John Hinckley's bullet bounced off the armored presidential limousine before striking him in the chest.

Reagan was especially adept at shrugging off embarrassing revelations, such as the news that his wife, Nancy, often dictated his travel schedule with the help of an astrologer. He even managed to elude responsibility for the

A Timeline of the 80s

1980

Operation Abscam, *a two-year sting operation in which FBI agents posing as Arab businessmen offered bribes in exchange for political favors, results in the indictment of one senator, seven congressmen, and 22 other government officials.*

The U.S. hockey team upsets the U.S.S.R. *at the Winter Olympics in Lake Placid, N.Y., on the way to a gold medal. In addition, speed skater Eric Heiden wins all five gold medals for his sport, a Winter Olympics record.*

A rescue mission *for U.S. hostages held in Iran is called off when two aircraft involved in the operation collide, killing eight crewmen.*

The Moscow Olympics *are boycotted by the United States and dozens of other nations to protest the Soviet invasion of Afghanistan.*

Toxic shock syndrome, *a sometimes fatal bacterial infection linked to women's use of superabsorbing tampons, leads to the recall of Rely brand tampons by Procter and Gamble.*

Teenage model Brooke Shields *appears in a Calvin Klein jeans commercial declaring, "You know what comes between me and my Calvins? Nothing." The spot is deemed too suggestive for TV.*

Ronald Reagan is elected president, *winning a majority of the popular vote over incumbent Democrat Jimmy Carter and independent John B. Anderson.*

The "Who Shot J.R.?" episode *of the popular prime-time soap opera "Dallas" draws a viewing audience of 83 million.*

Former Beatle John Lennon *is gunned down in front of his Manhattan apartment by Mark David Chapman, a mentally ill fan.*

Genetically engineered insulin *is successfully tested in humans with diabetes.*

New in print: *"The Official Preppie Handbook," edited by Lisa Birnbach; James Michener's "The Covenant"; Jean M. Auel's "Clan of the Cave Bear"; Joyce Carol Oates's "Bellefleur."*

New on TV: *Cable News Network; "ABC News Nightline"; "Magnum, P.I."; "Too Close for Comfort"; "Bosom Buddies."*

New products: *3M's Post-it Notes; cordless telephone; Rollerblades.*

The Academy Awards: *best picture—"Ordinary People"; best actor—Robert De Niro for "Raging Bull"; best actress—Sissy Spacek for "Coal Miner's Daughter."*

1981

The Iranian hostage crisis ends *after 444 days with the release of the 52 Americans held in Tehran.*

President Reagan is shot *and seriously wounded outside the Washington Hilton by John Hinckley Jr. Press Secretary James Brady and two escorts are also hit.*

Jean Harris, headmistress *of the Madeira School in Virginia, is convicted of killing Scarsdale Diet doctor Herman Tarnower.*

The first space shuttle, *the Columbia, blasts off from Cape Canaveral on its maiden voyage.*

Pope John Paul II is shot *and seriously wounded by Turkish radical Mehmet Ali Agca as he greets worshipers in Saint Peter's Square in Rome.*

AIDS (acquired immune deficiency syndrome) *is officially recognized by the U.S. government when the Centers for Disease Control publishes a report on the disease.*

Twenty serial murders *of black children and young adults in Atlanta, Georgia, are solved when Wayne B. Williams is arrested and charged in the 18-month reign of terror.*

worst White House scandal since Watergate—the illegal sale of arms to Iran and illegal diversion of the profits generated to aid the Contra rebels in Nicaragua. Reagan was "just like a Teflon frying pan," said Congresswoman Pat Schroeder of Colorado. "Nothing sticks to him."

A Simple Agenda. Not the least of Reagan's appeal was the straightforward simplicity of his political agenda. It was highly conservative and, in domestic matters, ran directly counter to nearly half a century of liberal policies. He declared, "We must balance the budget, reduce tax rates, and restore our defenses." He also advocated "getting the government off people's backs" by reducing federal regulations on the environment and business.

Reagan had hated high income taxes ever since his big-pay Hollywood days, when the top rate was 91 percent. As a presidential candidate, he seized upon a tax-cutting scheme called supply-side economics. According to this plan, tax reductions would stimulate the economy by providing incentives for investment, thereby generating so much growth—and hence new taxable income—that the government would actually gain revenue.

Critics labeled the idea "voodoo economics," a phrase coined, ironically, by Republican George Bush before he joined the Reagan ticket as vice presidential candidate. But in seven years Reagan and the Democratic Congress slashed the highest tax rate on even the richest Americans from 70 percent to 28 percent. At the same time Reagan, denouncing the Soviet Union as the "evil empire," pushed for the largest peacetime military buildup in U.S. history. Annual defense spending ballooned from less than $200 billion under Presidents Ford and Carter to nearly $300 billion in 1985. "America is back and standing tall," he proudly said of the newly strengthened armed forces.

The economy, pumped up by the tax cuts and increased military spending, soared in the longest peacetime expansion in U.S. history. Unemployment, which in Reagan's first year reached 10.7 percent, the highest since the Great Depression, shrank to about half that level by the end of his second term. Inflation plummeted from 12.5 percent to 4.4 percent. For the entire decade, the gross national product nearly doubled, and an estimated 20 million new jobs were created. By these measures, what had come to be known as Reaganomics was a roaring success.

But Reagan failed disastrously in his vow to balance the budget. In eight years he piled up more new federal debt than had accumulated in two centuries. The total red ink nearly tripled—to $2.6 trillion—on his watch. "Amer-

Sandra Day O'Connor, *shown here with Chief Justice Warren Burger, is named by President Reagan to be the first female Supreme Court justice.*

Lady Diana Spencer weds *Prince Charles, heir to the British throne.*

Striking air-traffic controllers *are fired en masse by President Reagan after defying a return-to-work order.*

Egyptian president Anwar Sadat, *62, is assassinated by rebel soldiers as he reviews troops in Cairo.*

New in print: *John Updike's "Rabbit Is Rich"; Leonard Michael's "The Men's Club"; John Irving's "The Hotel New Hampshire."*

New on TV: *Music Television (MTV); "Dynasty"; "Hill Street Blues"; "The Fall Guy."*

New products: *IBM personal computer; NutraSweet sugar substitute; Microsoft's MS-DOS; Chipwich; Pac-Man.*

The Academy Awards: *best picture—"Chariots of Fire"; best actor—Henry Fonda for "On Golden Pond"; best actress—Katharine Hepburn for "On Golden Pond."*

1982

Air Florida flight 90 crashes *into the Potomac River after taking off from Washington National Airport in a snowstorm, killing 77 people.*

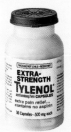

Cyanide-laced Tylenol capsules *kill seven people in the Chicago area, triggering a massive recall of the drug and nationwide concern about product tampering.*

The first permanent artificial heart *is given to Utah dentist Barney Clark, who survives for 112 days after the operation.*

Disney's EPCOT Center, *an $800-million futuristic theme park, opens in Orlando, Florida.*

America's first test-tube baby *is born to Judy and Roger Carr, stimulating a debate about ethical issues of in vitro fertilization.*

New in print: *Bruce Fierstein's "Real Men Don't Eat Quiche"; Alice Walker's "The Color Purple"; John Jakes's "North and South"; Paul Theroux's "The Mosquito Coast."*

New on TV: *"Family Ties"; "Cheers"; "St. Elsewhere"; "Late Night With David Letterman"; "Cagney and Lacey"; "TJ Hooker"; "Remington Steele"; "Newhart."*

New products: *Diet Coke; "USA Today"; Sony Watchman.*

The Academy Awards: *best picture—"Gandhi"; best actor—Ben Kingsley for "Gandhi"; best actress—Meryl Streep for "Sophie's Choice."*

1983

Singer Karen Carpenter dies *of a heart attack at age 32, calling attention to the serious consequences of such eating disorders as anorexia nervosa and bulimia.*

The Strategic Defense Initiative *(SDI), a plan for a space-based antiballistic missile system popularly known as Star Wars, is proposed by President Reagan.*

Astronaut Sally K. Ride *becomes America's first woman in space when she and four crewmates lift off aboard the space shuttle Challenger.*

More than 200 U.S. Marines are killed *as a truck bomb explodes outside their headquarters in Beirut, effectively ending the American attempt to keep peace between warring Muslims and Christians in Lebanon.*

Vanessa Williams *becomes the first African American to win the Miss America competition. Williams gives up her crown 10 months later when "Penthouse" magazine announces it will publish nude photographs of her.*

The United States invades Grenada, *a small Caribbean nation, after its prime minister is ousted during a bloody Marxist coup.*

ica has thrown itself a party," warned economist Benjamin Friedman, "and billed the tab to the future." But under Reagan Americans were more attuned to jazz singer Bobby McFerrin's bouncy little ditty, "Don't Worry, Be Happy."

"Greed is good." Reaganomics was largely responsible for touching off the biggest bull market in Wall Street history. Yet much of the financial frenzy had little to do with the kind of entrepreneurship that Reagan envisioned. Instead of investing in research, capital development, and higher productivity, many businessmen chose to devote their energy to mergers and takeovers. Using huge sums of borrowed money, corporate raiders bought out sound companies and then sold them off piece by piece to pay creditors and squeeze out a quick profit—typically at the cost of laid-off workers. In the movie *Wall Street,* the character named Gordon Gekko captured the new morality when he said, "Greed is good. Greed is right."

Gekko was loosely modeled after a central figure in the takeover boom, Ivan Boesky. The son of a Russian immigrant, Boesky was known as Ivan the Terrible for his relentless wheeling and dealing in the stocks of companies targeted for acquisition. His frequent business partner was Michael Milken, who pioneered the use of junk bonds—high-risk, high-yield corporate bonds—to raise billions of dollars to finance takeovers. Boesky and Milken often made more money in a few hours than most Americans would earn in a lifetime. In the end, however, both men went to prison and paid in fines much of their windfall after being convicted of insider trading and stock manipulation.

Despite his greed, junk-bond king Milken did not live extravagantly, which put him out of step with the rest of the decade's high rollers. Those who had it were expected to flaunt it. When Nancy Reagan decided the White House needed new china, she bought $200,000 worth, with private donations. Sales of stretch limousines doubled every year during Reagan's first term.

Pop demographers identified a new socioeconomic class infatuated with wealth and material possessions. These were the yuppies, an acronym that stood for young urban professionals. Yuppies of both sexes ate power lunches and "dressed for success" by wearing power suits. Hard-driving overachievers, they worked out in chic health clubs and either possessed or were seeking an MBA degree, which ostensibly stood for master of business administration but was widely held to mean "Making It Big in America."

Shopping malls, wrote one historian, had become "the cathedrals of American material culture." Surveys showed Americans spent more time

Lech Walesa, founder of Solidarity, *the Polish trade union, is awarded the Nobel Peace Prize for his efforts to gain the right for workers to organize freely.*

First Lady Nancy Reagan *launches an antidrug campaign featuring the slogan "Just Say No."*

New in print: *William Kennedy's "Ironweed"; Shirley MacLaine's "Out on a Limb"; Daniel Boorstin's "The Discoverers."*

New on TV: *"The A-Team"; "Hardcastle and McCormick"; "Scarecrow and Mrs. King"; "Night Court"; "Hotel."*

New products: *Trivial Pursuit board game; compact disk; Lotus 1-2-3 computer software; cellular phone network; computer mouse; contraceptive sponge.*

The Academy Awards: *best picture—"Terms of Endearment"; best actor—Robert Duvall for "Tender Mercies"; best actress— Shirley MacLaine for "Terms of Endearment."*

1984

Representative Geraldine Ferraro *of Queens, New York, becomes the first woman to run for vice president on a major-party ticket when Walter Mondale chooses her as his Democratic running mate.*

"Where's the beef?" *demands 83-year-old Clara Peller in popular TV commercials for Wendy's hamburger restaurant chain.*

A baboon heart is transplanted *into the body of 15-day-old "Baby Fae," sparking controversy among animal-rights activists, religious leaders, and medical scientists. She dies less than three weeks later.*

President Reagan and Vice President Bush *win reelection, carrying 49 states and posting the greatest Republican electoral-vote landslide in history.*

Bhopal, India, *experiences the world's worst industrial disaster as toxic fumes leak from a Union Carbide plant, killing more than 2,000 people.*

Genetic "fingerprinting," *the identification of an individual's unique DNA sequences, is developed by scientist Alec Jeffreys.*

New in print: *Jay McInerney's "Bright Lights, Big City"; Milan Kundera's "The Unbearable Lightness of Being"; Mark H. McCormack's "What They Don't Teach You at Harvard Business School."*

New on TV: *"The Bill Cosby Show"; "Miami Vice"; "Murder, She Wrote"; "Highway to Heaven."*

New products: *desktop laser printer; Chrysler minivan; Apple Macintosh computer; CD-ROM.*

The Academy Awards: *best picture—"Amadeus"; best actor—F. Murray Abraham for "Amadeus"; best actress—Sally Field for "Places in the Heart."*

1985

"We Are the World" *becomes an instant hit single after 45 rock, pop, and country music stars get together to cut the record as a fund-raiser for famine victims in Africa.*

Mikhail Gorbachev, *new Soviet leader, promises a policy of glasnost (openness) and an improvement plan called perestroika (restructuring).*

Coca-Cola introduces New Coke, *its first change in taste in 99 years. Just 10 weeks later, the company brings back the old version under the name Coca-Cola Classic in response to an avalanche of complaints from Coke lovers who prefer the original taste.*

Shiite Muslim terrorists *skyjack a TWA jetliner, killing one American and holding 40 others hostage in Beirut. After 17 days, the hostages are freed in exchange for the release of Lebanese detainees in Israeli prisons.*

The wreck of the Titanic *is discovered by a joint French-U.S. research team about 560 miles off the coast of Newfoundland.*

Limited economic sanctions *against South Africa are announced by President Reagan in response to that country's policy of apartheid.*

Pete Rose makes his 4,192nd hit, *breaking Ty Cobb's 57-year-old record for the most hits in a career.*

Country singer Willie Nelson *organizes the first Farm Aid concert to benefit farmers at risk of foreclosure.*

there than anywhere except home, job, or school. Much of what they shopped for—microwave ovens, VCRs, cordless phones—relied on the fingernail-size microprocessor chips that were transforming every facet of American life. Transcending all these prodigies of miniaturization was the personal computer, which in the 1980s became commonplace in homes and standard equipment in offices.

The Bad News. If heightened prosperity and a renewed national pride were the good news, there were also discouraging developments. The economic disparity between the haves and the have-nots deepened. Even the middle class shrank. In just five years 150,000 of the farmers who were central to Reagan's nostalgic vision of America went bankrupt. Most of Reagan's newly created jobs were in services, many of them positions in low-paying sectors such as fast food. Working-class families were often able to stay above water only because the wife took a job outside the home. By the end of the decade, maldistribution of income had reached the point that one-tenth of Americans controlled two-thirds of the nation's wealth.

And the poor got poorer. Partly as a result of federal budget cuts in food stamps, welfare, and Medicaid, the per capita income of the bottom 20 percent of American families actually dropped when adjusted for inflation. The bulge of population living below the poverty line broadened from 11.7 percent to 15 percent. One in five children was living in poverty—and too many of them were living on the streets. The number of homeless children and adults grew embarrassingly amid urban affluence and conspicuous consumption, reaching perhaps three million.

Many of the homeless were victims of something called "deinstitutionalization"—the well-intentioned policy that emptied out psychiatric hospitals but left thousands of former patients with no place to go and no ability to manage on the outside. Others were homeless because of cutbacks in federal housing assistance. Few appeared to fit into the category described by President Reagan in an offhand remark as "homeless, you might say, by choice."

Public health officials faced new problems of epidemic proportions. On the drug front, the hot new item was cocaine. An estimated 22 million Americans had tried the drug by 1982, though it was so expensive that actor Robin Williams quipped, "Cocaine is God's way of showing you were making too much money." Despite the dangers of addiction and other health problems, "coke" became the recreational drug of choice among Hollywood celebrities,

A hole in the ozone layer *is discovered in the atmosphere over Antarctica. The significance of the find would become a point of impassioned debate.*

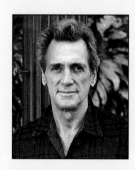

Actor Rock Hudson, *one of the first public figures to acknowledge his battle with AIDS, dies at age 59.*

New in print: *Anne Tyler's "The Accidental Tourist"; Oliver Sacks's "The Man Who Mistook His Wife for a Hat"; Garrison Keillor's "Lake Wobegon Days."*

New on TV: *"Moonlighting"; "Spenser: For Hire"; "The Equalizer"; "Dynasty II: The Colbys"; "The Golden Girls"; "Growing Pains."*

New products: *Microsoft Windows software; Pagemaker software; Nintendo Entertainment System; Ford Taurus.*

The Academy Awards: *best picture—"Out of Africa"; best actor—William Hurt for "Kiss of the Spider Woman"; best actress—Geraldine Page for "The Trip to Bountiful."*

1986

Martin Luther King Jr.'s birthday *is celebrated as a national holiday for the first time.*

The space shuttle Challenger explodes *73 seconds after liftoff from Cape Canaveral, killing all seven on board.*

The world's worst nuclear accident *occurs at a power plant in Chernobyl, Ukraine, U.S.S.R., killing at least 30 people and spreading radiation across northern Europe.*

The "Hands Across America" campaign *forms a human chain that reaches from Long Beach, California, to New York City and raises $100 million for the poor and homeless.*

Affirmative action hiring quotas *for minorities and women are upheld by the Supreme Court.*

The Iran-Contra affair, *the worst political scandal since Watergate, explodes when the Reagan administration acknowledges that the anti-Communist Nicaraguan forces called Contras were illegally given funds derived from an arms-for-hostages deal with Iran.*

Microsoft, *the computer software firm cofounded by Bill Gates, goes public, making him an instant $311 millionaire.*

Prince Andrew and Sarah Ferguson *of Great Britain say "I do," as do Tatum O'Neal and John McEnroe, Maria Shriver and Arnold Schwarzenegger, and Caroline Kennedy and Edwin Schlossberg.*

New in print: *Margaret Atwood's "The Handmaid's Tale"; Tom Clancy's "Red Storm Rising"; Robert Fulghum's "All I Really Need to Know I Learned in Kindergarten."*

New on TV: *"L.A. Law"; "Matlock"; "Alf"; "Perfect Strangers"; "Our World"; "Crime Story"; "The Oprah Winfrey Show."*

New products: *microwave pizza; nicotine chewing gum; Honda Acura; Polaroid Spectra; digital audiotape.*

The Academy Awards: *best picture—"Platoon"; best actor—Paul Newman for "The Color of Money"; best actress—Marlee Matlin for "Children of a Lesser God."*

1987

Tammy Faye Bakker *wipes a tear from her eye as she speaks out in support of her husband, former Praise the Lord (PTL) televangelist Rev. Jim Bakker, following revelations that he committed adultery and stole money from his ministry.*

The surrogate mother of "Baby M," *Mary Beth Whitehead, who contracted to be artificially inseminated by William Stern and then give the child to him and his wife, changes her mind and sues for custody of the child. A court awards full custody to the Sterns.*

Colorado senator Gary Hart, *a married man and 1988 Democratic presidential hopeful, is photographed rendezvousing with model Donna Rice. Hart withdraws from the race.*

Wall Street brokers, and athletes. One of the latter, University of Maryland basketball superstar Len Bias, had his life snuffed out by the drug just as he stood on the threshold of what promised to be a dazzling pro career.

In 1985, cocaine began to appear in a much cheaper and more highly addictive smokable form known as crack. The easy availability of this rocklike variant ravaged the urban ghettos. The federal government launched a "war on drugs," and Nancy Reagan headed up the campaign to "just say no."

The other major new public health problem was AIDS. Although the first cases of acquired immune deficiency syndrome were reported in 1981, the gruesome disease did not become the focus of national attention—and fear—until four years later, when it killed actor Rock Hudson. The Hollywood star had been a friend of the Reagans, but the president generally ignored the disease, which struck hardest at male homosexuals and intravenous drug users. He did not even mention AIDS in a public speech until 1987. Two years later, hundreds of thousands of Americans were thought to be infected with the AIDS virus, and more than 50,000 had died because of it.

Conservative Backlash. Old perils and new ones threatened the environment. The biggest oil spill in U.S. history befouled the wildlife and pristine waters and shoreline of Alaska's Prince William Sound after the tanker *Exxon Valdez* ran aground. Scientists warned about newly discovered ecological threats. Above Antarctica a hole the size of the U.S. reportedly had opened in the ozone layer, which shields the earth from dangerous ultraviolet rays. Smoke from coal-fired power plants in the Midwest wound up as acid rain falling on the lakes and forests of the northeastern United States and Canada.

The Reagan administration tended to ignore these new dangers while busily rolling back enforcement of existing environmental regulations. Reagan's first secretary of the interior, James Watt, had served as legal counsel for western business interests dedicated to private development of federal lands. Watt eased restrictions on strip mining, leased federal preserves to mining companies at bargain-basement rates, and opened up vast expanses for offshore oil and gas exploration.

Other social and political movements that had gained momentum in the previous two decades also felt a conservative backlash. Reagan and his allies opposed two key civil rights initiatives—busing to integrate public schools and affirmative action. The women's movement suffered setbacks as well. In 1982 the proposed Equal Rights Amendment to the Constitution fell

Lieutenant Colonel Oliver North *appears before a House panel investigating the Iran-Contra affair and asserts that his covert actions were fully justified for national security reasons and were authorized by his superiors.*

Nazi war criminal Rudolf Hess, *Adolf Hitler's former deputy, hangs himself at age 93 in West Berlin's Spandau Prison after 46 years in custody.*

"Baby Jessica" McClure, *an 18-month-old who fell down an abandoned well in Midland, Texas, is rescued while millions watch on TV.*

On "Black Monday," *October 19, the Dow Jones Industrial Average plunges 508 points, the largest decline since 1914.*

The INF Treaty (on intermediate-range nuclear forces) is signed. This agreement between the Soviet Union and the U.S. eliminates all ground-launched nuclear missiles with a range of up to 3,400 miles.

The California Raisins, products of a new animation process called claymation, sing "I Heard It Through the Grapevine" in a TV commercial and become an instant hit.

New in print: Toni Morrison's "Beloved"; Scott Turow's "Presumed Innocent"; Randy Shilts's "And the Band Played On"; Tom Wolfe's "Bonfire of the Vanities."

New on TV: "thirtysomething"; "Teenage Mutant Ninja Turtles"; "Married . . . With Children"; "A Different World"; "Beauty and the Beast"; "Jake and the Fatman."

New products: disposable camera; Prozac antidepressant; soybean milk; Macintosh II and SE computers.

The Academy Awards: best picture—"The Last Emperor"; best actor—Michael Douglas for "Wall Street"; best actress—Cher for "Moonstruck."

1988

Jimmy "The Greek" Snyder, a CBS sports commentator, is fired after he tells a television reporter that "the black is a better athlete to begin with because he's been bred to be that way."

Televangelist Jimmy Swaggart tearfully confesses before a crowd of 6,000 to an unspecified sin.

The U.S. cruiser Vincennes mistakes an Iranian civilian airliner for a warplane and shoots it down, killing all 290 passengers.

Used needles and vials of blood, some of which test positive for the AIDS virus, wash up along Long Island's southern shore.

The savings and loan crisis comes into focus as experts estimate that it will cost as much as $200 billion to bail out hundreds of federally insured financial institutions that have overextended themselves.

U.S. swimmer Matt Biondi wins five gold medals and teammate Janet Evans wins three at the Summer Olympics in Seoul.

The Reverend Jesse Jackson makes a strong bid for the Democratic presidential nomination, transforming the position of black Americans in national politics.

Junk-bond broker Michael Milken is cited for two counts of insider trading by the Securities and Exchange Commission.

The space shuttle Discovery launches successfully, putting the nation back into space for the first time since the 1986 Challenger explosion.

George Bush and Dan Quayle are elected president and vice president, defeating Democrats Michael Dukakis and Lloyd Bentsen with 53.9 percent of the popular vote.

Pan Am flight 103 explodes over Lockerbie, Scotland, killing all 259 aboard. Investigators later confirm that the explosion was caused by a terrorist bomb.

three states short of the 38 needed for adoption. Another key tenet of feminism—the right to choose abortion—came under growing attack from forces that called themselves prolife.

At the same time, however, individual blacks and women scored important breakthroughs. Sandra Day O'Connor was named to the U.S. Supreme Court by Reagan in 1981. In 1983 Sally Ride became the first woman astronaut, followed two months later by the first African American in space, air force lieutenant colonel Guion Bluford. In 1988 the Reverend Jesse Jackson made a serious run for the Democratic presidential nomination, gaining the second highest number of votes in the primaries. Geraldine Ferraro became the Democratic candidate for vice president the same year. A year later, African American Douglas Wilder was elected governor of Virginia, once the home of the Confederate capital. Also in 1989, General Colin Powell became the first black chairman of the Joint Chiefs of Staff. The decade's two leading TV personalities were Oprah Winfrey and Bill Cosby.

End of an Empire. The decade's most far-reaching events took place in the nations dominated by the Soviet Union since World War II. The precise role played by Reagan's massive defense buildup in these developments would become the subject of fierce debate. But the man who set them in motion was the Soviet premier, Mikhail Gorbachev. Soon after he rose to power in 1985, Gorbachev unleashed radical reforms on the stagnating Soviet system. His policy of *glasnost* (openness) brought new freedom of speech; his *perestroika* (restructuring) nudged the Soviet Union in the direction of a free market. Gorbachev also negotiated missile-reduction agreements with Reagan.

Then, while Reagan's successor, George Bush, watched from Washington in fascination and disbelief, the Soviet leader stunned the world by relinquishing control over Eastern Europe—control that had long been a drain on the failing Soviet economy. In June 1989, just when the Communist Chinese government was cracking down on protesters rallying for democratic reform in Beijing's Tiananmen Square, Gorbachev was bringing home the Red Army.

Without Soviet tanks to protect them, Communist dictators soon fell to democratic forces in Hungary, Poland, Czechoslovakia, and Bulgaria. In November 1989, less than two months from the end of the decade, East Germans broke free and accomplished what liberty-loving people everywhere had never expected to see. The Berlin Wall—that hulking symbol of Soviet oppression—came tumbling down.

New in print: *Gabriel García Márquez's "Love in the Time of Cholera"; Stephen Hawking's "A Brief History of Time"; Anne Tyler's "Breathing Lessons."*

New on TV: *"Murphy Brown"; "Roseanne"; "The Wonder Years"; "Dear John . . ."; "Midnight Caller"; "Wiseguy"; "In the Heat of the Night."*

New products: *Disposable contact lenses; Rogaine hair restorative; Doppler radar.*

The Academy Awards: *best picture—"Rain Man"; best actor—Dustin Hoffman for "Rain Man"; best actress—Jodie Foster for "The Accused."*

1989

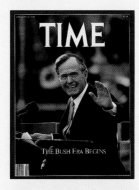

George Bush is inaugurated *as the 41st president of the United States.*

Author Salman Rushdie *is placed under a threat of death by Iran's Ayatollah Khomeini for allegedly insulting Islam in his new novel "The Satanic Verses."*

The tanker Exxon Valdez runs agrounds *in Prince William Sound, Alaska, dumping 11 million gallons of crude oil into the water.*

The U.S. invades Panama *after Manuel Noriega usurps the presidency. Noriega eventually surrenders and is later convicted in a Florida court of drug trafficking, money laundering, and racketeering.*

In Beijing's Tiananmen Square, *a young political protester becomes a world-renowned icon of physical and moral courage as he faces down a column of tanks. The army subsequently fires into a crowd of students demonstrating for reform; estimates of the number killed range from several hundred to several thousand.*

A Robert Mapplethorpe photography exhibit, *funded by the National Endowment for the Arts, draws harsh criticism from members of Congress for its homoerotic and sadomasochistic content. The show, scheduled for Washington's Corcoran Gallery of Art, is canceled.*

General Colin Powell *becomes the first African American chairman of the Joint Chiefs of Staff.*

Texas Ranger Nolan Ryan *becomes the first pitcher in major-league history to strike out 5,000 batters.*

Pete Rose *is banned from baseball and ruled ineligible for the Hall of Fame for betting on major-league games.*

Billionaire hotelier Leona Helmsley *is convicted of income-tax evasion, including illegal deductions for girdles, and sentenced to four years in jail plus a fine of $7.1 million.*

Hurricane Hugo *pummels the Carolinas, killing more than 70, leaving thousands homeless, and causing approximately $4 billion in damage.*

The "World Series" earthquake, *measuring 7.1 on the Richter scale, strikes northern California, causing widespread destruction in the San Francisco Bay area, including the collapse of the upper deck of a freeway bridge in Oakland, which kills more than 40 people in their cars.*

L. Douglas Wilder *becomes the nation's first elected black governor in Virginia—once the heart of the Confederacy.*

The Berlin Wall falls, *and hundreds of thousands of East Germans stream into democratic West Berlin as the 40-year-old East German Communist government collapses.*

The U.S. soccer team *beats Trinidad and Tobago 1-0, winning a berth in the final round of the World Cup for the first time since 1950.*

New in print: *John le Carré's "The Russia House"; Amy Tan's "The Joy Luck Club"; John Grisham's "A Time to Kill."*

New on TV: *"The Arsenio Hall Show"; "Life Goes On"; "Coach"; "Anything but Love."*

New products: *Mazda Miata; computer screensaver "Flying Toasters."*

The Academy Awards: *best picture—"Driving Miss Daisy"; best actor—Daniel Day-Lewis for "My Left Foot"; best actress—Jessica Tandy for "Driving Miss Daisy."*

Imagemakers
Extraordinaire

★

EIGHT FOR THE 80S

When Oprah Winfrey hauled a little red wagon heaped with lard before the cameras on her November 15, 1988, talk show to publicize her weight loss, the stunt confirmed that the main subject of *The Oprah Winfrey Show* was Oprah Winfrey. But most of her viewers knew that already, and they were eager for more.

Getting the skinny on celebrities became an American obsession in the '80s. Whether it was a fixation on the newlywed Princess Diana's storybook life or admiration for Meryl Streep's virtuoso acting, whether one swore by clergyman Jerry Falwell's politically tinged fundamentalist Christianity or followed with fascination the revolutionary TV entrepreneurship of Ted Turner, the unprecedented convergence of the private and the public cast the luminaries of the decade in a glaring light. Winfrey, by turns sisterly, sassy, and confiding, found no topic unfit for this new tell-all etiquette. The "first lady of talk shows" was unfazed by live births on her program, white supremacists, transsexuals, even tales of incest (of which she herself was once a victim). "The first day I did it," she said of her talk-show career, "I thought, 'This is really what I should have been doing all along.' "

Something else was new in the world of celebrity: Alongside Winfrey, Jesse Jackson in politics, Bill Cosby in family entertainment, and Michael Jackson in music helped make it clear that being one of America's favorite personalities was no longer solely a white prerogative.

Having shed 67 pounds in five months, an exuberant Oprah Winfrey—sporting size 8 jeans—pumps up her studio audience in 1988. Just four months after going national her talk show was rated number one.

I always felt very different from everyone else, very detached. I knew I was going somewhere different but had no idea where.

So he said, "Will you marry me?" and I laughed. I remember thinking, "This is a joke," and I said: "Yeah, OK," and he laughed. He was deadly serious. He said: "You do realize that one day you will be Queen." And a voice said to me inside: "You won't be Queen, but you'll have a tough role." So I thought, "OK," so I said: "Yes." I said: "I love you so much, I love you so much." He said, "Whatever love means." . . . So I thought that was great! I thought he meant that! And so he ran upstairs and rang his mother.

One minute I was a nobody, the next minute I was Princess of Wales, mother, media toy, member of this family, and it was just too much for one person to handle.

I desperately loved my husband, and I wanted to share everything together. I thought we were a very good team.

The first foreign trip we took William to Australia and New Zealand. That was for six weeks. That was great—we were a family unit. It was very tricky, mentally, for me, because the crowds were just something to be believed. My husband had never seen crowds like it and I sure as hell hadn't and everyone kept saying it will all quieten down when you've had your first baby, and it never quietened down, never.

People think that at the end of the day a man is the only answer. Actually, a fulfilling job is better for me.

I think the biggest disease this world suffers from [is] people feeling unloved. I can give love. . . . I'm very happy to do that, and I want to do that.

However bloody you are feeling, you can put on the most amazing show of happiness.

A Fantasy Come to Life

Call it a fairy-tale wedding or a royal spectacle, the marriage of Lady Diana Frances Spencer and Charles Philip Arthur George, the Prince of Wales and heir to the British throne, was the kind of love story Hollywood no longer made, the kind of grand costume pageant it could no longer afford to produce.

She was a "distinctively dishy commoner"—as *Time* magazine put it—the radiant 20-year-old bride who would become the most photographed and gossiped-about personality of her time. He was her Prince Charming. On July 29, 1981, before two million on-the-scene witnesses and an avid television audience of three-quarters of a billion around the world, reality seemed to outshine fantasy.

From the time Charles began courting her, Diana captured and held the relentless and fevered attention of the world press. "You didn't know," the royal watcher at London's *Daily Mirror* once asked her, "you were marrying us too?" Not only her marriage but her exercise routines, eating habits, hair styles, and wardrobe became daily fodder for a hungry public.

While acting the part of poised princess, doting mother, and good-will ambassador, Diana struggled to maintain some semblance of a private life and keep the spotlight away from her two sons—William (born June 1982) and Harry (born September 1984), irreverently dubbed "an heir and a spare" by the papers.

Eventually Diana's media stardom, perceived by many to have been achieved at her husband's expense, opened up fault lines in their picture-perfect marriage. "With the media attention came a lot of jealousy," she once confessed, "and a great deal of complicated situations arose because of that." On one embarrassingly public occasion a grimy, sweaty Charles kissed her after a 1986 polo match, and Diana was photographed wiping her lips with the back of her hand.

By the end of the decade, it was clear that the prince and princess were not living happily ever after. And although the public's fascination with Diana, who began the decade as a shy country girl and ended it as an international celebrity, was still growing, her fame would soon be tinctured with disfavor.

Looking fetchingly demure despite her glamorous evening gown and pearl choker, Princess Diana casts a doe-eyed glance sideways at a 1981 London gala.

My constituency is the desperate, the damned, the disinherited, the disrespected and the despised.

I was born against the odds. I grew up against the odds. I stand here against the odds. I am an odds breaker and a dream maker. I will never surrender.

America is not like a blanket. . . . It is more like a quilt—many patches, many pieces, many colors, many sizes, all woven together by a common thread. The white, the Hispanic, the black, the Arab, the Jew, the woman, the Native American, the small farmer, the businessperson, the environmentalist, the peace activist, the young, the old, the lesbian, the gay and the disabled make up America's quilt.

We can move from the slave ship to the championship! From the guttermost to the uppermost! From the outhouse to the courthouse! From the statehouse to the White House!

If in my low moments, in word, deed, or attitude, through some error of temper, taste, or tone, I have caused any discomfort, created pain, or revived someone's fears, that was not my truest self. As I develop and serve, be patient. God is not finished with me yet.

The language of [black] culture grows out of our Christian faith. We gained strength from biblical heroes and heroines. . . . People who don't understand my language—I am speaking English—are culturally deprived. . . . When I give the example of rocks lying around and ask people to pick up their slingshots and throw their rocks, I'm not talking about hitting somebody. Blacks understand that I'm telling them to register and vote.

Whether I win or lose, American politics will never be the same.

Apostle of a Party of Many Colors

Life's greatest tragedy, the Reverend Jesse Louis Jackson had always taught his children, was "not failure but a low aim." Now, standing before the 1988 Democratic National Convention, Jackson was living out that philosophy. "Our time has come!" he declaimed, his voice and his charisma punctuating a dramatic lift in the hopes of his people. In the person of Jackson, for the first time in history, an African American had been a realistic candidate for—indeed, had barely missed—a major-party presidential nomination.

The illegitimate son of a South Carolina high-school student, Jackson had become a bold and articulate fighter against injustice. From his early civil rights work with Dr. Martin Luther King Jr. and his days in Chicago in the 1970s as the founder of Operation PUSH (People United to Save Humanity), he evolved to become the embodiment of black pride and a major actor on the national stage.

First in 1984, and then even more successfully in 1988, Jackson took his newly formed National Rainbow Coalition—a multiracial alliance of the underprivileged and the disenfranchised—and brought their dreams to the brink of reality, outrunning a slew of well-established white political rivals along the way.

Using an oratorical style rich in metaphor and biblical allusions, he collected 3.5 million votes (as many as two million of them newly registered) in the 1984 Democratic presidential primaries, campaigning on a budget of less than $3 million. "If Hart and Mondale had my budget," he said of his two major rivals, "they could not compete." In 1988, Jackson was even more formidable, garnering nearly seven million votes in Democratic primary elections across the country as he finished second to Massachusetts governor Michael Dukakis.

"After traveling this country in two presidential campaigns and getting seven million votes," he declared upon his move from Chicago to Washington, D.C., in early 1989, "I have earned the right to be part of the national governing body." No one, black or white, could argue with that.

A stirring orator, Jesse Jackson (right) outran five of six white rivals for the Democratic presidential nod in 1988, powerfully boosting black political clout.

To act upon one's convictions while others wait,
To create a positive force in a world where cynics
abound,
To provide information to people where it wasn't
available before,
To offer those who want it a choice;
For the American people, whose thirst for under-
standing and a better life has made this
venture possible;
For the cable industry, whose pioneering
spirit caused this great step forward in
communications;
And for those employees of Turner Broadcasting,
whose total commitment to their company has
brought us together today,
I dedicate the News Channel for America—
The Cable News Network.
—Dedication of CNN, June 1, 1980

*I'm going to do news like the world has never
seen news before. This will be the most significant
achievement in the annals of journalism.*

*We are at war with everybody. Now we have
lawsuits against the three networks, the White
House, and Westinghouse. And we're winning—
or at least we haven't lost yet.*

My desire to excel borders on the unhealthy.

*I want to live in five lives. I have to hurry to get
them all in.*

*I am not worried about what people think. I
am the right man in the right place at the right
time, not me alone, but all the people who
think the world can be brought together by
telecommunications.*

*I've got everything I need personally. I've got a
baseball team, a basketball team, a soccer team,
two 60-foot yachts, a plantation, a private island, a farm, a wife, five kids, and two networks.
Ain't never been anybody in the history of the
world ever had more than me. So let me tell you
what I'm going for. I'm going now for the history
books. I'm swinging for the fences.*

An Openly Ambitious Man

He was known as "the Mouth from the South," "Captain Outra-geous," and, after recovering from financial troubles in the mid-1980s, "Captain Comeback." Ted Turner, by almost any set of standards, was as original, enterprising, belligerent, and self-indulgent a man as America had ever produced.

He made himself into a media kingpin and even skippered an Amer-ica's Cup-winning yacht. *Time* declared him "perhaps the most openly am-bitious man in America." And by the end of the '80s he was also one of the richest, presiding over an empire worth a staggering $5 billion.

In business Turner was a gambler, and his biggest gamble seemed, at first, a reckless one: a 24-hour news channel on the fledgling medium of cable TV, where he had launched his "Superstation" WTBS in 1976. Cable News Network (CNN) got off to a slow and error-filled start on June 1, 1980, but within two years it was reaching 13.9 million living rooms. It pro-vided live, round-the-clock coverage through satellite uplinks, giving view-ers a dramatic and irresistible window on the news as it unfolded. Turner's claim that he had created "the most significant achievement in the annals of journalism" took on an aura of truth.

With breakneck speed Turner's network was on the scene for the decade's biggest stories—the shooting of President Reagan in March 1981, the explosion of the space shuttle *Challenger* in January 1986, the May 1989 student uprisings in Tiananmen Square, the fall of the Berlin Wall in November of that year. Frequently beating the big three networks to the punch, CNN provided exhaustive, eyewitness coverage no mere half-hour news broadcast could hope to match, although, as a 24-hour medium, it sometimes struggled to hold its audience when little was happening.

As the '80s came to a close, CNN and a new sibling network, CNN Headline News, were reaching 51 million homes in the United States and countless others in 83 nations abroad. In addition, Turner's empire had ex-panded to include such holdings as Turner Entertainment, which syndicat-ed MGM movies, and the new Turner Network Television—TNT—as well as the Atlanta Braves baseball team and basketball's Atlanta Hawks. "It's ob-vious I was seeing things that other people didn't see," said Turner, "just like Columbus discovered the world was round."

Seemingly taking himself in from the vantage point of a TV screen, the energetic Ted Turner finds a rare moment to stand still. "All my life," the successful entrepreneur declared in 1984, "people have said I wasn't going to make it."

Racial humor was about 35 percent of my act when I first started. But I realized that it was a crutch. What brought it home to me was when another comedian said to me, "If you changed your color tomorrow, you wouldn't have any material." He meant it as a put-down, but I took it as a challenge.

I don't think you can bring the races together by joking about the differences between them. I'd rather talk about the similarities, about what's universal in their experience.

All parents experience the same problems. Does it mean only white people have a lock on living together in a home where the father is a doctor and the mother is a lawyer and the children are constantly being told to study by their parents?

When you're younger, you want to be sure that by the time you're 80 years old you can sit on the bench and look back and say, "Man, I did it all. I didn't miss a thing." What you never meant to do was to hurt anyone, but then you see the look on the face of the person you didn't mean to hurt, and then you realize that what you stand to lose is worth so much more.

Why should I go out there and say, "Ladies and gentlemen, I grew up in a Negro neighborhood?"

My wife and I have four more children to, hopefully, put through college. Our first one has chosen a school that costs $13,000 a year. Four times $13,000 is $52,000. Add another $30,000 . . . for incidentals, and my wife and I will have spent over $82,000 to watch our daughter pick up a degree in liberal arts, which qualifies her to come back home.

In America . . . the seven ages of man have become preschooler, Pepsi generation, baby boomer, mid-lifer, empty-nester, senior citizen, and organ donor.

America's Funniest and Richest Father

When Bill Cosby's best-selling book, the warm and funny collection of observations called *Fatherhood,* made him America's most famous dad in 1986, he was on a roll. He had already established himself as the country's most beloved and best-paid entertainer. By the end of the decade, in fact, Cosby was nothing less than an industry, the man who simultaneously brought the black middle class to the acme of prime-time television and propelled his own fame—and earnings, estimated at $57 million in 1987 alone—into the stratosphere.

Like Ronald Reagan, another entertainer with a warm, fatherly image, Cosby shaped a message of optimism and traditional family values into an American success story. *The Cosby Show* debuted on September 20, 1984. The bearers of its upbeat, family-first message were unprecedentedly—and unstereotypically—African American. The show's main characters, Cliff and Claire Huxtable, like Cosby and his real-life wife, Camille, were college educated, financially successful, and the parents of five children. "I got tired of seeing TV shows that consist of a car crash, a gunman and a hooker talking to a black pimp," Cosby said. "It was cheaper to do a series than to throw out my family's six TV sets." Thanks to Cosby, other Americans were glued to their sets in record numbers: Midway through its first season, *The Cosby Show* was enjoying the highest ratings in television history.

The show's essentially color-blind approach to life, replete with what *Life* magazine called "the delicious ordinariness of its pleasures," offered a welcome respite from the racial turbulence and mutual mistrust of the '60s and '70s. In a decade when most Americans wanted to feel good, it gave them a very good reason to do just that.

When, by 1987, reruns of *The Cosby Show* had earned a record $600 million and *Fatherhood* had sold nearly three million copies in hardcover, America's funniest father, the man NBC chairman Grant Tinker called "the 800-pound gorilla of television, an absolute giant," had quite a bit to feel good about as well.

Perturbed, attentive, good-natured, and amazed by turn, Bill Cosby's whimsically expressive face (right) was one of the nation's most recognizable during the 1980s.

If the leaders of Christendom in the nation don't stand up against immorality, we can't expect anyone else to lead. I believe it is the duty of gospel preachers to set the pace. When sin moves to the front, preachers and Christians everywhere must speak out. I will as long as I have breath.

I could care less what Walter Cronkite thinks of me, or Jimmy Carter, or people like that. I didn't care before, I don't care now, I won't care tomorrow. I'm not running for anything, so they can't affect my support. My grass roots people are with me. Most important, I think God is with me. So I don't get up in the morning and think about my critics.

After I had settled in my own heart that it was possible to be involved in political and social issues as a Bible-believing Christian without violating the Bible that I believe and love, the job was now clearly to begin the task of creating . . . a "moral majority."

We are pro-life, pro-traditional, pro-moral, and pro-American.

I am often charged with trying to establish a Christian America. I don't want a theocracy, but yes, I would like more people in this country to live Christian lives.

It was the American people, not the Moral Majority, who elected Ronald Reagan . . . but we helped.

If God will give us the time, I believe that— through the 110,000 fundamentalist churches, the 34,000 Christian day schools, and dozens of Christian colleges and universities across this country, and hundreds of TV and radio outlets and preachers and programs, and Christian businessmen, we can turn this nation to God.

The whole world loves us or hates us, and the rest are scared of us.

Silver-Tongued Oracle of the Christian Right

Religion and politics marched down the aisle in the 1980s, and the man largely credited with performing the marriage was televangelist Jerry Falwell. From his base of operations at the Thomas Road Baptist Church in his hometown of Lynchburg, Virginia, Falwell's fundamentalist *Old Time Gospel Hour* had been beamed every Sunday evening since the early '70s to nearly two million households. By the dawn of the '80s he recognized the political potential of his televised ministry and launched the organization he confidently named the Moral Majority to "reverse the politicization of immorality in our society."

His timing couldn't have been better. The 1980 Republican presidential candidate, Ronald Reagan, agreeing with the organization's stands on school prayer and abortion, received the support of Falwell's well-financed outfit. Without the help of the Moral Majority, said pollster Lou Harris, "Reagan would have lost the election by one percentage point."

Falwell had precisely the right qualities for making a success of a TV ministry. He was congenial yet earnest, confident yet humble, reasonable yet morally righteous—what *Time* referred to as an "artful entrepreneur in rube's clothing." His preachings awakened in the public deep-seated feelings on abortion, homosexuality, pornography, education, and feminism, and by mid-decade was raising more than $100 million a year in the process. "We want to be part of society without endorsing all the philosophies and lifestyles of that society," Falwell declared. Enough Americans agreed that not only U.S. politicians but international figures, from South African prime minister P. W. Botha to members of Israel's religious right, heeded his opinion, as he covered over 8,000 miles a week in an Israeli-built jet purchased by the church.

By 1989, however, televangelism was reeling from scandals involving some of Falwell's fellow TV ministers, and the squeaky-clean leader of the Moral Majority dissolved the organization. Despite this setback, a biographer's claim that "Falwell has altered the terms of political discourse in this country" was true beyond any disputing.

The Reverend Jerry Falwell (right) pulled no punches on the pulpit: "If a man stands by this book," he said about the Bible, "vote for him. If he doesn't, don't."

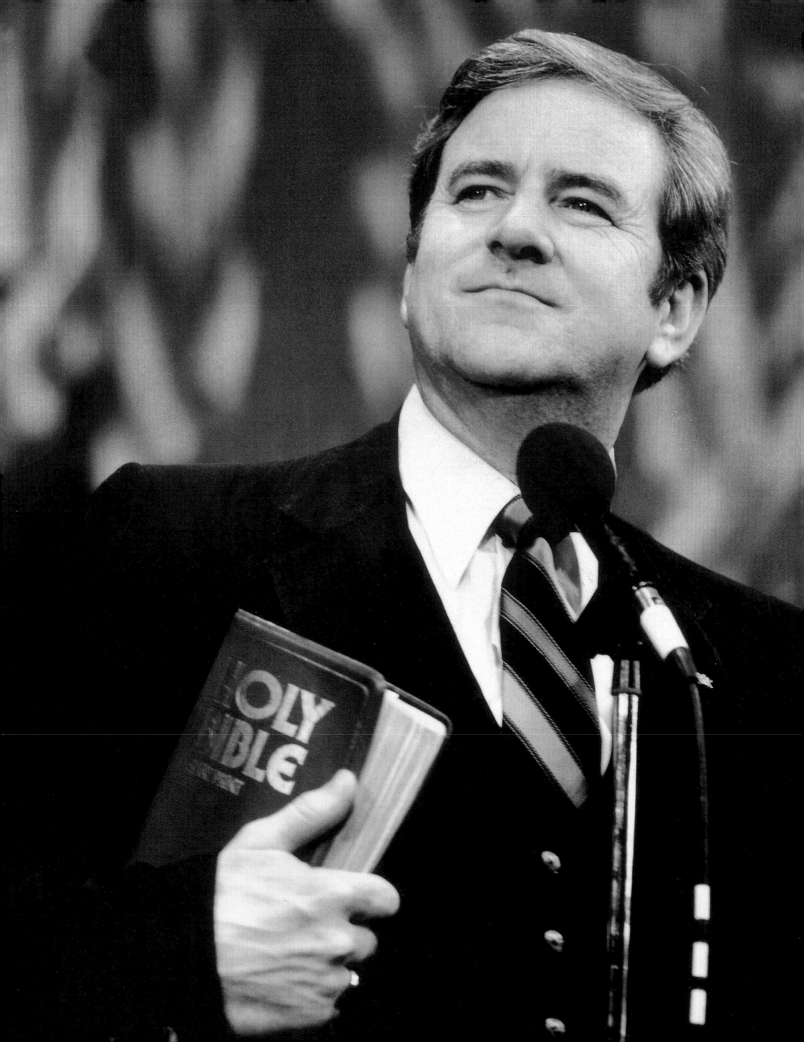

Enchantress of Stage and Screen

When Meryl Streep, to the alarm of her director, seemed to slip into a comalike state while playing a gutter-bound derelict in the 1987 film *Ironweed,* she was only doing what came naturally: becoming her character. With a malleability bordering on the magical, Streep, described by *Silkwood* costar Cher as "an acting machine in the same sense that a shark is a killing machine," created perhaps the most diverse gallery of female characters in American cinematic history.

From the beguiling Sarah Woodruff in *The French Lieutenant's Woman* to the aristocratically romantic Baroness Blixen in *Out of Africa* to the raunchy, blue-collar whistle-blower in *Silkwood,* Streep used her remarkable beauty and skill at mimicking accents to become what one critic called "one of the great enchantresses, a creature of mystery who haunts our dreams." Over the decade, Streep garnered six Oscar nominations, winning the best actress award for *Sophie's Choice* in 1982 and giving, said *Time,* "new life to a cinema starved for shining stars."

I have no Method, you know. I've never read Stanislavsky. I have a smattering of things I've learned from different teachers, but nothing I can put into a valise and open it up and say, "Now which one would you like?" Nothing I can count on, and that makes it more dangerous. But then the danger makes it more exciting.

It's the great gift of human beings that we have this power of empathy. We can all feel like Elliott when E.T. died. We can all cry for each other. We can all sense a mysterious connection to each other. And that's good. If there's hope for the future of us all, it lies in that.

It's fun to re-create those feelings—and not have any of the repercussions. Just think of what lives I've lived vicariously. I've been poisoned by radiation, sent a child to the gas chamber, lost custody of another, lost husbands and lovers. God! If it weren't for the moments when I fell in love, I'd go nuts!

Exposing one of her "quasi-Mongolian cheekbones," as Life magazine put it, Meryl Streep (right) strikes a pensive pose, her face capable of animating any part.

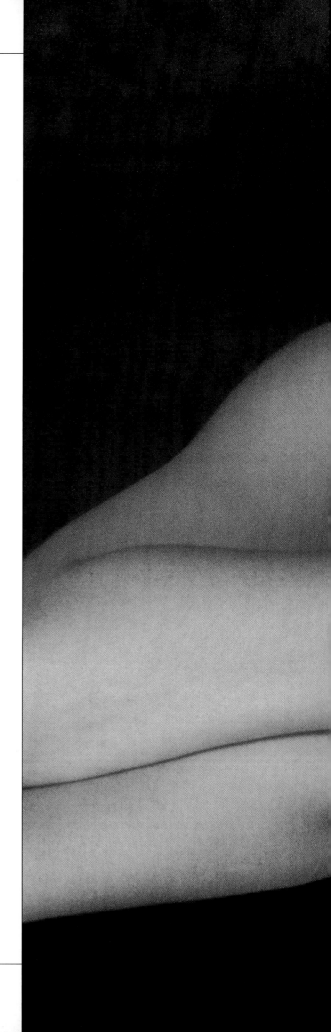

*Michael's got a fresh original sound. The music
is energetic, and it's sensual. You can dance to it,
work out to it, make love to it, sing to it. It's
hard to sit still to.*
—Jane Fonda

*He seems partly child, partly adult, partly mas-
culine, partly feminine; he seems to be a person
for all ages and all sexes. I don't see that he is
doing any harm, but I'm not sure he's doing any
good either.*
—Dr. Benjamin Spock

*If E.T. hadn't come to Elliott, he would have
come to Michael's house.*
—Steven Spielberg

*My Lord, he's a wonderful mover. He makes
these moves up himself and it's just great to
watch. Michael is a dedicated artist. He dreams
and thinks of it all the time.*
—Fred Astaire

*like the old Indian proverb says
Do not judge a man until you've walked
2 moons in his Moccosins.
Most people don't know me, that is why they
write
such things in wich MOST is not TRUE
I cry very very often Because it Hurts and I
wory about the children all my children all over
the
world, I live for them.
If a Man could say nothing AGAINST a
character but what he can prove, HISTORY
COULD
NOT BE written.
Animals strike, not from malice, But because they
Want to live, it is the same with those who
CRITICIZE, they desire our BLOOD, not our
pain. But still I must achieve I must seek
Truth in all things. I must endure for the power
I was sent forth, for the world for the children
BUT HAVE Mercy, for I've been Bleeding a
long time now.*
—Michael Jackson, published in *People* magazine,
   November 12, 1987

Thriller

With music that combined equal parts soul and show-biz glitz, Michael Jackson moonwalked his way to being the biggest and flashiest performer in recorded music. His 1982 megahit album *Thriller* won an unprecedented eight Grammy awards, blending high-tech acoustic effects and Jackson's strong tenor with vocal stunts such as squeals, gasps, and even hiccups.

Contributing to the worldwide *Thriller* hysteria was Jackson's groundbreaking work on what was to be the entertainment phenomenon of the '80s: the music video. Videos had been made before, primarily to help sell records, but Jackson burst onto the screen with a cast of 200, turning the rock dance tune "Beat It" into a stylized street fight between rival gangs. The video clips of the three number one singles from *Thriller* —the title track, "Beat It," and "Billie Jean"—were lauded by the *Village Voice* as "the state-of-the-art last-word new thing in rock video."

Jackson set new standards not only in video choreography but on the stage as well. Biographer Albert Goldman described the lithe, five-foot-10-inch mover and shaker as "so graceful he can transmute a ghetto handslap into a gesture of kinesthetic beauty . . . so fast, he makes your eyes blur."

In November 1984 Jackson became the subject of the first issue of *People* magazine ever to be devoted entirely to one person. This even though the musical wunderkind with the trademark sequinned white glove and spindly, androgynous beauty refused to be interviewed. "On-stage," Jackson once explained, "I feel so free, so unlimited. . . . When I'm not onstage, I'm quiet and shy. I sort of close down."

In 1987 Jackson released his next album, *Bad,* which produced five chart-topping singles and sold 20 million copies—numbers that would put into orbit any career except his. *Thriller* had been so revolutionary, and had sold in such historic numbers, that any follow-up was doomed to look diminished by comparison.

By the decade's end the performer's intersexual looks, peculiar habits, bizarre tastes, and rumored interest in young boys began to eat away at his public image and provoked him to respond *(letter, bottom left).* Michaelmania, inevitably, had subsided.

Michael Jackson (right) mesmerized his audience onstage and in music videos shown on MTV. Time magazine characterized him as "eroticism at arm's length."

It's Morning Again in America

★

A FRESH BREEZE FROM MOVIELAND

N ever had the country experienced an inaugural like Ronald Reagan's in 1981. For a start, there was its extravagance: the biggest fireworks display; the most celebrants at the most glittering balls; the most stars of stage and screen performing, partying, and creating the worst traffic jams of the most limousines ever seen in Washington. "This is the first administration to have a premiere," quipped Johnny Carson.

Contrasted with all the merrymaking was the persistent uneasiness of many Americans, worried about the economy and grappling with the incongruity of a one-time B-movie actor in the nation's most important job. But then came electrifying news. Minutes after Reagan took office, Iran released the 52 American hostages it had held for 444 days *(pages 118-119)*. Suddenly America's long humiliation was over, swept away by a sense of jubilant relief combined with a surge of patriotism and national confidence.

The new president pledged to cut taxes, subdue the continuing double-digit inflation, get the economy growing, and strengthen the military to win the Cold War. Popping jelly beans from the stein on his Oval Office desk *(inset)*, Reagan achieved those ends, though at great cost to future generations saddled with a national debt that almost tripled during his two terms. Voters seemed not to mind. They gave him the highest popularity ratings of any president since polling began in the 1930s.

President-elect Reagan radiates winning good cheer. "What I'd really like to do," he once said, "is go down in history as the president who made Americans believe in themselves again."

Roles of a Lifetime, On and Off the Screen

I n Reagan's life, where movies and reality sometimes appeared to swap places, the role of president seemed one he was born to play—an affable hero rising from humble roots to the top. Son of an Illinois shoe salesman whose drinking kept the family on the edge of poverty, young Ronald acquired from his mother a cheerful confidence he never

Reagan, only 21 in this publicity photo for his first radio job, already shows winning charm.

> **"Some day when things are rough and the breaks are going against the boys, ask them to go in there and win one for the Gipper."**
>
> Ronald Reagan as the dying George Gipp in *Knute Rockne—All American*

lost. After graduating from Peoria's Eureka College in 1932, he became a radio sports announcer. His first movie role? Radio announcer, in 1937.

The handsome six-footer's engaging screen personality won him B-movie roles and a few parts in better pictures. The ex-college footballer landed the role of varsity hero George Gipp in 1940's *Knute Rockne—All American*. His poignant death scene in that film made him a star.

But in the early 1950s his movie career waned, and he became a television spokesman for General Electric *(left)*. Increasingly conservative in his views, he astonished America in 1966 by winning election as California's governor, a job he held for two terms. During his first campaign, a reporter asked how well he would do in the post. "I don't know," Reagan replied with self-effacing humor. "I've never played a governor."

Reagan donned six-guns in the 1953 flick *Law and Order (above, middle)*. In 1957's *Hellcats of the Navy*, he played opposite his wife, Nancy Davis.

As "the Gipper" in Knute Rockne, Reagan boots a punt down the field. He got the part, his most memorable role, only by showing producer Hal Wallis photos of himself in his old Eureka College football uniform.

A Mad Deed That Shook the Nation

Scarcely two months after Reagan took office, on March 30, 1981, John W. Hinckley Jr. watched from a crowd as the smiling president crossed a Washington sidewalk to his limousine. Then the young man fired six shots from a .22-caliber pistol. Instantly, Secret Service agent Jerry Parr pulled down Reagan's arm *(left)* and shoved him into the car, which sped away. At first nobody knew the president had been hit. Reagan thought the agony he soon experienced and the blood he spat resulted from Paar's leaping protectively on top of him in the limousine. In fact, a ricochet off the car had entered Reagan's body beneath his raised arm.

"Honey, I forgot to duck."

Ronald Reagan to Nancy, borrowed from boxer Jack Dempsey, to his wife after losing a title fight in 1926

The shooting had lasted only two seconds. But in that time, Hinckley had put not only a bullet into Reagan's lung but another into the brain of his press secretary, a third into the abdomen of a Secret Service man trying to block the shots with his body, and a fourth into the neck of a Washington policeman. No one died, but the event was like a blow to the gut of assassination-weary America.

Reagan played the scene for laughs. His one-liners, passed on to the public from his hospital bed, calmed the nation. He asked a female emergency-room nurse who gently held his hand, "Does Nancy know about us?" To surgeons about to operate: "Please tell me you're Republicans." Reagan was back at work within a month, his support from the country newly cemented by his courage and humor.

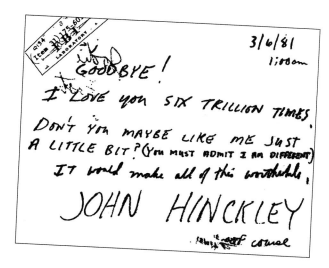

A note from Hinckley shows his obsession with actress Jodie Foster, who did not know him. In another, written an hour before the shooting, he said he planned "to get Reagan" and added, "At least give me the chance with this historical deed to gain your respect and love." Seized immediately, Hinckley was later judged insane.

Press Secretary Jim Brady, who sustained severe brain damage in the shooting, sprawls facedown on the sidewalk, a policeman's dropped revolver by his head. At left rear lies Secret Service agent Timothy McCarthy, who took a bullet in the midsection.

A President You Could Count On

When, in 1981, air-traffic controllers on an illegal strike refused an order to return to work, Reagan agreed with Transportation Secretary Drew Lewis's decision to fire them. "Drew, don't worry about me," Reagan said when Lewis called to reaffirm the president's backing. "When I support someone—and you're right on this strike—I'll continue to support you, and you never have to ask that question again."

Reagan's ability to make a decision, stick to it, and delegate the authority to carry it out was just one of the reasons his leadership worked well. Another was his willingness to bargain. "I've never understood people who want me to hang in there for 100 percent or nothing," he said. "Why not take 70 percent or 80 percent, and then come back another day for the other 20 percent or 30 percent?" He was called the Great Communicator because he could convey major ideas in simple terms, illustrated by anecdotes from life or the movies. He revised his speechwriters' work, inserting or emphasizing the ringing lines his audiences loved. And the public liked what he did, approving even a bombing raid against Libya in 1986 to punish dictator Muammar al-Qadhafi for the terrorist bombing of a Berlin discotheque frequented by American soldiers in which one GI was killed.

But the simplicity of thought that gave his speeches such clarity could obscure gradations of understanding and his perception of events in the shadows. He was grateful, for example, that Franklin Roosevelt's Depression policies had rescued his parents from poverty, yet he seemed to regard 1980s social programs as boondoggles for the lazy. He saw government as inherently flawed; he and his team were there to fix the problem. He was blind to chicanery from his own people so widespread that "the sleaze factor" became a journalistic byword in discussions of his administration. When the head of the Justice Department's criminal division argued that Attorney General Edwin Meese should be indicted for corruption, the president refused, sticking by his man.

Reagan often seemed a stranger to anxiety. He worked hard, but rarely late. "A great many evenings," he told reporters, "you'll find Nancy and me in pajamas and a robe having dinner, and then early to bed." There were, however, some events so painful and problems so perplexing (*overleaf*) that they surely kept him awake at night.

"The President has a unique talent: He is serene internally. When he makes a decision, he lives with it. He doesn't fret over it. And most of all, he doesn't change his mind."

Donald Regan, Reagan's chief of staff, 1986

Reagan and British prime minister Margaret Thatcher trade thoughts while walking at Camp David in 1986 (opposite). Thatcher said Reagan enlarged "freedom the world over at a time when freedom was in retreat."

Tragic Deaths and Illegal Doings

A t 6:20 a.m. on Sunday, October 23, 1983, most of the 300 U.S. Marines in the barracks at Beirut's airport were still in bed when a yellow pickup truck turned into the parking lot. Even as a sentry raised the alarm, the truck accelerated and smashed into the barracks lobby. There it exploded with the force of six tons of TNT, collapsing the four-story structure and killing 241 marines.

It was the biggest U.S. military loss since Vietnam, and for Reagan, the most painful event of his presidency. "Sending the Marines to Beirut," he later wrote, "was the source of my greatest regret and my greatest sorrow as President." He had dispatched 800 leathernecks to Lebanon in August 1982 for "three or four weeks" to help a multinational force try to end the vicious civil war raging there.

After the bombing, Reagan insisted that the U.S. could not "turn tail and leave"; to do so would only encourage terrorism. But pressured by Congress and the public, he pulled the troops out in February 1984 and declared that

At left, marines search desperately for comrades, injured or dead, in the wreckage of their Beirut barracks. Later, President and Mrs. Reagan mourn the fallen at a rainy memorial service (above) at the Camp Lejeune, North Carolina, marine base.

> "A few months ago I told the American people I did not trade arms for hostages. My heart and best intentions still tell me that's true, but the facts and evidence tell me it is not."

Ronald Reagan, March 4, 1987

any blame for the disaster "rests . . . with this president."

Reagan felt less responsible for the worst debacle of his presidency—a tangle of illegal acts and lies, many under oath, perpetrated by some of his closest aides and known as the Iran-Contra affair. The administration had illegally sold weapons to Iran for money and the promise to release hostages kidnapped in Lebanon by terrorists under Iran's control. Part of the money went to buy weapons for Nicaraguan rebels known as Contras—Reagan called them "freedom fighters" for their efforts to topple Nicaragua's Communist dictatorship—even though Congress had expressly prohibited arming them. Two of Reagan's national security advisers, Robert McFarlane and John Poindexter, plus marine colonel Oliver North, who managed the scheme, were later convicted of numerous crimes. In the end, none of the major players went to prison, but McFarlane became despondent and attempted suicide.

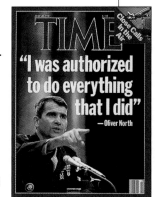

Three investigations never settled whether Reagan had approved the illegal acts. To his mind, he had not. Oliver North later claimed that Reagan had known everything all along (inset). In any case, the "Teflon president" emerged from Iran-Contra, as he had from the Beirut bombing, without serious political damage.

At Last, a Chance for Peace

At the Geneva summit of November 1985 Ronald Reagan and Soviet general secretary Mikhail Gorbachev met face to face for the first time. "Here we were, I said, two men from humble beginnings," Reagan later recalled. "Now we were probably the only two men in the world who could bring about World War III. At the same time, I said, we were possibly the only two men who might be able to bring peace to the world."

"Trust but verify."

Ronald Reagan

Reagan wanted a treaty; Gorbachev was wary. He balked at the Reagan administration's continuing research into the Strategic Defense Initiative—space-based weapons able to destroy missiles as they lifted from their silos. But the two leaders kept talking, and on December 8, 1987, they signed a treaty in Washington *(inset)* that called for the destruction of all intermediate-range missiles, those that could hit targets from 300 to 3,400 miles away. For the first time, an entire class of weapon, comprising 1,752 Soviet and 830 American missiles, disappeared from the earth.

Reagan left office before agreement could be reached on other force reductions. But he had fulfilled his pledge to win the Cold War. His military buildup helped persuade the Soviets, whose economy could not support an arms race, to end the contest. By 1990 most of Eastern Europe had slipped from Russian control and the Berlin Wall had tumbled *(pages 136-137)*.

Solemn faces alternate with smiles at a White House welcoming ceremony the day before the world's two most powerful leaders signed a treaty to abolish intermediate-range missiles.

A Spectrum of Lifestyles

★

When the Reagans moved into the White House in 1981, their air of unabashed affluence sent a clear signal that the gloomy Carter years were over and prosperity and high style were back. As inflation and interest rates fell and the stock market turned bullish, the country responded, adopting an upbeat attitude. "Shop till you drop" became a catch phrase. Yuppies sought out everything from pricey real estate to the grown-up toy of the moment—such as Rubik's Cube *(inset)*—while parents lined up to buy Cabbage Patch Kids, computer games, and other hot new playthings. Designer clothing and celebrity fashions set style trends, but some young Americans went their own way: "Punks," mostly white kids, wore deliberately outlandish getups; fans of rap music, mostly black, adopted the hip-hop look of the performers.

For many Americans life wasn't complete without the sleek good looks and sense of well-being that came with a high state of physical, mental, and spiritual fitness. They paid extravagant fees to go to posh health clubs and spas that offered not only basic conditioning but an amazing array of feel-good extras.

Much of the country's exuberant spending on lifestyle was done with credit cards. But such high living could not go on forever, and late in the decade a Wall Street collapse *(pages 96-97)* put a crimp in the rambunctious '80s.

Supermodel Christie Brinkley exemplifies the '80s ideal of tautly sculpted, athletic beauty. Helped by the decade's penchant for glamour and glitz, her work earned her as much as $6 million a year.

LONG SHADOW BOOKS
47684·X
$4.95

THE YUPPIE HANDBOOK

The State-of-the Art Manual for Young Urban Professionals

Marissa Piesman and Marilee Hartley

Pin Stripe Suit

Cross Pen

Sony Walkman

Rolex Watch

Ralph Lauren Suit

Squash Racquet

Cartier Tank Watch

Burberry Trench Coat

Coach Bag

Gucci Briefcase

Fresh Pasta

Co-op Offering Prospectus

Gourmet Shopping Bag

Running Shoes

L.L. Bean Duck Hunting Boots

Rolex watch

Cuisinart food processor

Alessi teakettle

By 1984 yuppies had become such a well-established phenomenon that they had even acquired their own instruction manual (left). Marissa Piesman and Marilee Hartley published this tongue-in-cheek guidebook presenting rules for living the yuppie lifestyle, such as what to wear, what car to drive, where to vacation, and even what foods to eat.

Catalogs

Nouvelle cuisine

Bottled water

BMW sedan

The Rise of a New Social Class

Early in the decade a new demographic group emerged—"young urban professionals," or yuppies. Well-educated baby boomers between 25 and 35, yuppies were dedicated to achieving happiness through money and possessions. "We were upper-middle-class white kids who were used to getting what we wanted," recalled James Kunen, a former student radical-turned-lawyer.

Yuppies streamed from their suburban breeding grounds into the cities, transforming run-down districts into upscale neighborhoods in a process called gentrification. Wearing clothes bearing designer labels *(inset),* poring over catalogs of prestige products *(left),* they gathered just the right accouterments— Rolexes, Cuisinarts, BMWs, Jacuzzis. To satisfy their lust for *things,* they frequently went heavily into debt.

Dedicated to career advancement, yuppies often treated leisure time as an extension of work—a membership at an exclusive fitness club, for example, provided a chance to "network." They dined out often, spurring a boom in trendy restaurants. By 1988, however, drawing criticism for their seemingly shallow, materialistic values, maturing yuppies gravitated toward home ownership and children, trading their BMWs for minivans and their champagne dinners for gourmet carry-out.

American punks took much of their style from the British punk rockers of the mid-1970s. Their attention-getting fashions were usually as far removed from the conventional as possible, calculated to shock and irritate their elders.

Outlandish "Punks"

Like the hippies of the '60s, punks rejected the values of a culture they perceived to be materialistic and hypocritical. But lacking the optimism of hippies, they withdrew from the world rather than trying to change it. Bereft of a unifying ideology, punks defined themselves in terms of what they were not. As one youth aptly stated, "I don't have much use for the Left or the Right, they both want to *make me behave!*"

In an attempt to distance themselves

"What we all have in common is some kind of anger."

Natalie Jacobson, age 20

---

from mainstream society, punks made themselves appear as unapproachable as their imaginations could manage. They pursued any style they felt would be shocking or distasteful to the straight world. Boys and girls often sported identical wardrobes as they sought an androgynous look. Typically between 13 and 21 years old, punks made involvement in the music scene a central focus of their lives, keeping apprised of local events through "fanzines," underground newsletters created by enterprising and articulate punk writers and artists.

A poster boy for punk, this young man flaunts tattoos, body piercings, chains, grungy clothing, and a radical hair style to shout out loud his disdain for the culture that engendered him.

Toys and Technology

Transformers

Cabbage Patch Kids

BABY ON BOARD!

Retail sales of playthings in the U.S. hit a record $13.4 billion as the decade fostered one kids' craze after another. Youngsters could choose from an impressive assortment of products at every level of sophistication, from simple figurines to complex computer games *(pages 84-85)*. Still prized by the younger set after more than two decades, Mattel's Barbie doll appeared in new Hispanic, African American, and Asian versions. Teddy Ruxpin, a talking teddy bear, became a huge favorite, his speech produced by a built-in microchip.

Low-tech Cabbage Patch Kids were a surprise hit, projecting an irresistible appeal as "orphans" who had been born in a cabbage field and coming with an "official" adoption certificate. The frenzy for Kids during the 1983 Christmas season led to parental desperation; one man even flew to London to buy a doll for his daughter. And as children became a predominant concern among maturing baby boomers, the yellow "Baby on Board" sign *(inset)* appeared in thousands of car windows across the nation.

MASTERS OF THE
UNIVERSE®

Smurfs

Skateboarding, a fad from
the '60s, experienced a
resurgence in popularity.
The new generation of
skateboarders wore hel-
mets and protective
padding as they executed
daredevil flips and twists
on specially designed
courses.

My Little Pony

Strawberry
Shortcake
lunchbox

Teddy Ruxpin

Spas that offered warm mud baths became meccas for adventurous health seekers. Bathers extolled the merits of the slippery sludge, good for everything from drawing out toxins and releasing tension to promoting a youthful appearance.

Fitness and the Feel-Good Industry

Exercise became a national obsession in the '80s. Health clubs, once the domain of sweaty weightlifters and avid basketball players, now attracted wealthy executives and professionals of both sexes, all striving to attain a bodily ideal. "Fitness is another way of signaling to people that you are serious," said 24-year-old banker Joseph Barron.

Clubs offered Nautilus rooms, aerobics classes, racquetball courts, and added enticements like saunas, tanning beds, and massage. Memberships in glitzy establishments could cost as much as $2,000 a year.

Joggers and bicyclists coursed down streets and through parks in pursuit of fitness. In living rooms and dens, Raquel Welch, Arnold Schwarzenegger, and other celebrities led sweating viewers in videotaped workouts, promising them glamorous, muscular bodies, while Richard Simmons *(inset, top)* cried, "Tuck in those *tushies,* girls!" The undisputed queen of the exercise video was Jane Fonda *(inset, bottom),* who trailed only Nancy Reagan and Sandra Day O'Connor among the most influential women in America, according to the 1984 *World Almanac.*

Workout attire was important. Sexy spandex leotards, bodysuits, and tank tops replaced gym shorts and T-shirts; leg warmers and workout sneakers were essential accessories. Catalogs offered whole lines of exercise garb for the discriminating devotee, and sales of activewear skyrocketed.

Another facet of the fitness craze was a growing interest in holistic health, and "wellness" became the buzzword of its proponents. The concept began with stress reduction, proper nutrition, and emotional balance, but health spas also offered programs on relaxation, time management, diet, and improving personal relationships, as well as herbal wraps, mud baths, aromatherapy, massage, and other trendy natural treatments. Most spa-goers loved the pampering, although one complained, "One day on the diet, I was ready to devour the raspberry shower gel."

Star-Power Fashions

The '80s ushered in a mélange of fashions, many of them inspired by the outfits worn by pop stars and characters in hit movies and TV series. Madonna *(right, top)* performed in a dizzying array of costumes, starting fads among "wannabes"—her young female fans. To their parents' dismay, wannabes wore sexy lace tops, chains, wooden-cross earrings, and torn fishnet stockings like those Madonna displayed in her videos or her 1985 movie, *Desperately Seeking Susan.*

Epitomizing the laid-back flair of TV's hippest cops was Don Johnson *(inset)*. His "Miami Vice" look, which took off with the popularity of that show, was based on Italian men's fashions. Macy's set up a Miami Vice section in its young men's departments, and apparelmakers jumped on the bandwagon with formalwear and shoes named after the series.

Young women didn't have to work up a sweat to emulate Jennifer Beals's casual air in the movie *Flashdance (opposite)*. Ripping the collar of a sweatshirt, cutting off the sleeves, and perhaps pulling on several pairs of socks would do the trick.

Don Johnson of Miami Vice popularized pastel suits worn with T-shirts, no socks, and a three-day stubble.

From thrift-store chic (above) to Hollywood glamour, Madonna changed styles as readily as a chameleon changes color.

In the 1983 coming-of-age movie Risky Business, Tom Cruise made a huge new hit of an old product, Ray·Ban "Wayfarer" sunglasses.

Jennifer Beals, star of the film Flashdance, *inspired the hardworking dancer look—off-the-shoulder sweater over tank top, tightfitting pants, and, often, leg warmers.*

Athletes' Endorsements

Many sports superstars were famous beyond the playing field or ball court. Their faces also came into millions of living rooms plugging some brand of shoe, beer, or breakfast cereal on TV. In ever growing numbers, athletes of the '80s hired agents not only to land them good playing contracts but also to sign them up for high-paying advertising deals. The money from some stars' product endorsements actually exceeded what they earned for playing their sport.

Even amateur athletes entered the world of advertising. Long forbidden to make money from their sport, in 1984 they were given free rein to capitalize on their fame when the International Amateur Athletic Federation and the International Olympic Committee ruled that they could finance their training and living expenses through product endorsements.

Jim Palmer

Sports figures like Michael Jordan, Carl Lewis, Jim Palmer, Boris Becker, Wayne Gretzky, and Mary Lou Retton recommended everything from the sporting equipment they used to soft drinks and mutual funds, testifying, "You know, you can work up one heck of a thirst on the pommel horse. . . ." or "It isn't easy being No. 1. But there's one mutual fund that has been No. 1 longer than any other. . . ."

Air Jordan shoe

Members of the rap group Heavy D and the Boyz sport hip-hop hair styles. The performers on the left and right wear "fade" cuts with designs at the bottom; the one in the center has baby dreadlocks. Hip-hoppers often shaved nicknames or symbols into their hair.

Below, the rap group Salt-N-Pepa models some of hip-hop's fashions, including African-style caps, gold chains, and athletic jackets. Female rappers sometimes wore bodysuits, tights, or even bathing suits under oversize jackets or shirts.

From the 'Hood to the World

The hip-hop culture of the '80s had its roots in rap music, which began in the '70s in African American neighborhoods of New York City. The music gained wide popularity after the 1979 hit "Rapper's Delight," by the Sugar Hill Gang. To achieve the unorthodox sound, rap DJs used multiple turntables and mixers to combine songs, rotate records forward and backward ("scratching"), and repeat selected fragments ("sampling"). Grandmaster Flash, the Einstein of rap, explained, "I couldn't bear just sitting there waiting for the record to end, so I started inventing tricks." The DJs accompanied the music with a syncopated spoken patter—the rap—a style that originated in African American folk games. Break dancing, a product of hip-hop, grew out of African and Caribbean dance techniques. Doing head spins, one-armed rotating handstands, and jump splits, break dancers often competed with each other to see who could make the most spectacular moves.

Teens across the nation enthusiastically adopted hip-hop's music and dancing as well as its styles. The hooded sweatsuits, oversize jeans, baggy shorts, and backward caps worn by fans of hip-hop gradually filtered into the world of high fashion.

Wearing protective gloves and an elbow pad, a break dancer performs before a wall spray-painted with graffiti, hip-hop's signature art form.

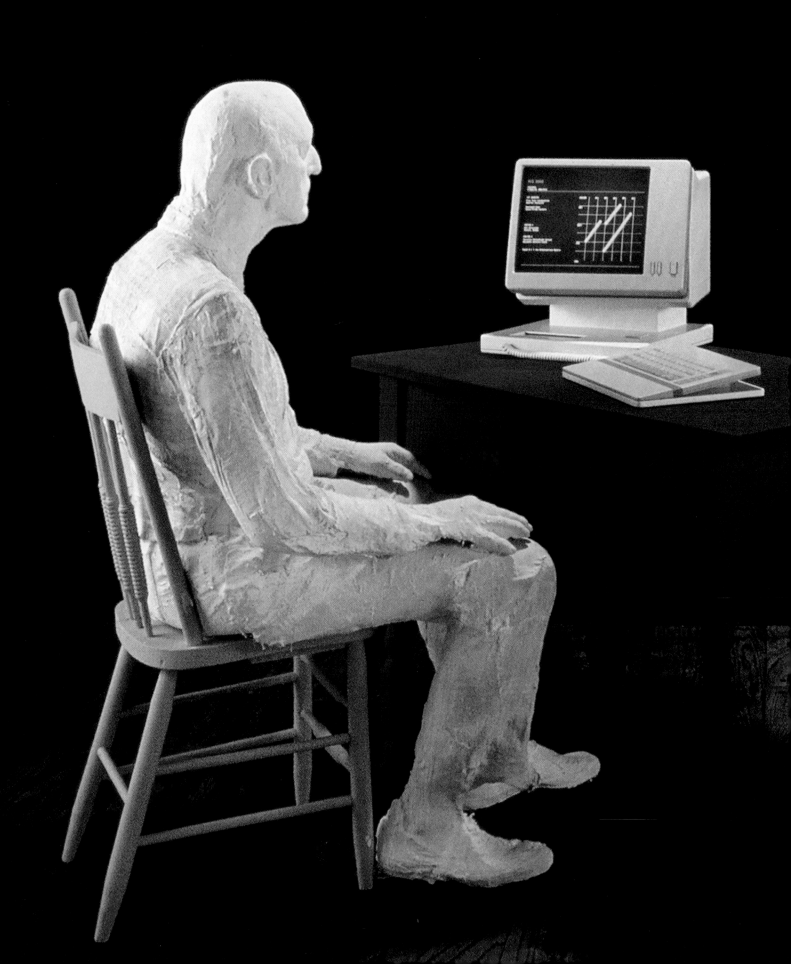

A Desktop Revolution

★

THE RISE OF THE PC

H ello, I am Macintosh," said the little machine in an electronically generated voice when it was unveiled at Apple Computer's annual shareholders' meeting in January 1984. "Unaccustomed as I am to public speaking, I'd like to share with you a maxim I thought of the first time I met an IBM mainframe: Never trust a computer you can't lift!" Letting a computer speak for itself was deft theater, but what the audience loved most was the sassy tone, perfect for an industry that characterized itself as a revolution in progress.

It was hard to argue with that assessment, for the 1980s saw the personal computer go from a mere glimmer in the eye of hobbyists to a fixture in offices, homes, schools, and many other spheres of human activity. The one-person, one-computer phenomenon had such a powerful impact that it was made the subject of a *Time* magazine cover in 1983.

As with all revolutions, this one had a lengthy gestation. A key event was the invention of the transistor, a sandwich of semiconducting material such as germanium or silicon, by Bell Laboratory scientists back in 1947. Transistors were to prove faster and far more reliable than the vacuum tubes then in use, and they also opened the way to astonishing miniaturization: By the end of the 1960s the basic circuitry of a general-purpose computer could be etched on a single tiny chip of silicon—the microprocessor *(inset)*.

Although the chips led to faster and less massive computers, the machines remained large and expensive, intended for big jobs such as solving scientific problems, wading

A personal computer holds center stage in this sculpture rendered for the January 3, 1983, cover of Time. In a first, Time declined to choose a Man or Woman of the Year, instead naming the PC Machine of the Year.

Bill Gates (left) was 19 and Paul Allen 21 when they produced the first commercial software for personal computers in 1975.

The Altair 8800, shown here with a precursor in a spoof of "socialist" art, launched the age of personal computers in 1975. When introduced, it had toggle switches instead of a keyboard for data input; indicator lights displayed results.

through vast thickets of data, or managing a payroll. Typically, they occupied an air-conditioned room and were tended by a priesthood of technicians.

Many users fantasized about having a scaled-down computer of their own, but IBM and other industry leaders disdained the idea. Then, more as an act of financial desperation than anything else, a small outfit in Albuquerque decided to give it a try. In the January 1975 issue of *Popular Electronics,* the company, Micro Instrumentation and Telemetry Systems—MITS, for short—introduced the Altair *(left, bottom).* Heretofore hobbyists had, from time to time, managed to patch together a string of circuits that might pass for a personal computer, but the Altair kit made the job much easier, and at a bargain price of just $397.

The Altair was a primitive affair, lacking both keyboard and monitor, but these and other add-ons could be attached. As for software— the instructions given to a computer to enable it to function—operators were expected to write their own, using a customized version of a language called BASIC. Sold along with the Altair, BASIC was the creation of Harvard sophomore Bill Gates and Paul Allen, Gates's childhood buddy, then working as a programmer in Boston *(left, top).* Convinced that personal computers were the coming thing and that software—heretofore traded freely among hobbyists— could be valuable property, they formed a partnership called Microsoft and used their modest payments from MITS as a grubstake for further programming ventures.

Within months, the country's first computer stores opened to sell the Altair. The device was, as one buyer remembered, "an absolute runaway, overnight, insane success." MITS didn't have the market to itself for long, however. Commodore International made heavy inroads with a bare-bones machine it called PET (for Personal Electronic Transactor). Tandy RadioShack came out with a computer that included a keyboard, a monitor, and a storage device. But the entry that quickly eclipsed all others came from a pair of young hackers whose ideas of success involved aesthetics and personal fulfillment as much as profit: Steve Jobs and Steve Wozniak *(opposite, top).*

Jobs and Woz, as Wozniak was called, grew up in the area south of San Francisco that would be later be dubbed Silicon Valley. Woz loved to design elegant circuitry. Jobs, four years younger, had experimented with drugs, traveled to Asia to learn about Eastern religions, and dropped out of Reed College in Oregon after a year. Back in California, he lived at home, designed video games for Atari, and joined Wozniak—then working at electronics giant Hewlett-Packard—to build gadgetry for hitching illegal rides on the telephone system.

Both of them attended meetings of a local organization called the Homebrew Computer Club, formed right after the announcement of the Altair. At club gatherings, the membership—a loose group of electronics enthusiasts—swapped technical gossip, exchanged pieces of hardware, and dreamed aloud about an age of individual computing. "There was a strong feeling that we were subversives," one member said about the Homebrew spirit. "We were subverting the way the giant corporations have run things."

In early 1976 Jobs and Wozniak arrived at a Homebrew meeting toting a clunky-looking piece of gear they had built in their home workshop. When they started it up for a demonstration, all the circuits blew. Despite that inauspicious beginning, they went on to sell a few of the computers. Soon their obvious talents—Wozniak as a designer, Jobs as a driven, mesmerizing salesman—attracted backing from a venture capi-

Steve Jobs (left) and Steve Wozniak, drawing on their respective gifts for salesmanship and circuit design, scored big with the Apple II.

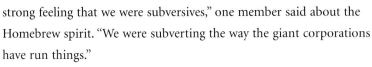

"There was a strong feeling that we were subversives."

Homebrew Computer Club member

talist for their budding enterprise, which they named Apple Computer.

By the following year they had made a huge leap forward, introducing a little dazzler called the Apple II—and a lively logo *(inset)* to go with it. Priced at $1,298, the 12-pound machine, which had a keyboard molded into a sleek plastic case and used a TV set for a monitor, could do a great many things—perform complex financial calculations at lightning speed, run circles around a typewriter, manipulate all kinds of data, play games, and much more. Adding further utility, in 1978 Apple—and Tandy RadioShack—introduced a drive for a 5.25-inch floppy disk *(inset, page 80),* making it easy to store and transport data. Sales of

Apple IIs travel down a production line in 1981. Apple Computer continued to turn out improved versions of this popular machine until 1986.

Elaine Ng, age five, taps at a computer at her Dallas school in 1982. PC makers offered low-cost programs to get their products into schools and win the loyalty of future customers. By 1989 almost 40 percent of all American students also had access to a computer at home.

The IBM PC (left) and the Apple Macintosh were the top contenders for personal-computer leadership in mid-decade.

the Apple II soared. By 1982 Apple Computer did $583 million worth of business. The two Steves were very, very rich.

Meanwhile, mighty IBM was finally waking up to this new phenomenon. Big Blue set up a team to build a machine of its own. The designers were given a degree of independence that was, for the normally uptight IBM, unprecedented, and they took full advantage of it. They cut costs by using components made by other manufacturers, and—in what some IBMers regarded as an even more shocking break with corporate tradition— they disclosed the operational details of the machine, thus allowing anyone to write software for it.

The most critical piece of software was the operating system, a set of instructions that orchestrated the computer's internal workings. In 1980, IBM acquired a system from Gates and Allen's Seattle-based Microsoft. As part of the deal, Microsoft retained the right to license the system—called MS-DOS, for Microsoft Disk Operating System—to any other computer maker. That clause would prove staggeringly profitable to Microsoft.

5.25-inch floppy disk

The IBM PC, which came with a keyboard, a monitor, two disk drives, and a then-impressive 256 kilobytes of memory, uncorked a gusher of profits after its introduction in mid-1981. To Big Blue's dismay, however, a large chunk of the bonanza soon began going elsewhere. Competitors found ways to get around IBM's flimsy copyright protection, and the market became flooded with "IBM clones," which sold for considerably less than the original and could use all the thousands of software programs written for it.

High-flying Apple was running into problems, too. A successor to the Apple II flopped. Then came an ambitious offering called Lisa— named for Jobs's baby daugh-

ter—which popularized a stunning new approach to computing.

Formulated at the Xerox Corporation's Palo Alto Research Center, a kind of think tank for improved office technology, the new system was called, among other names, the graphical-user interface, or GUI (pronounced "gooey"). It offered the operator an alternative to punching sequences of keys to give commands to the computer. With GUI the commands were displayed on the screen, and the operator, using a device called a mouse, could simply move an on-screen pointer to the desired command and click a button on the mouse to execute the command.

Digital watch

Steve Jobs recognized the revolutionary impact of this new approach and embraced it fervently, hiring away a score of Xerox employees to begin building an Apple version for Lisa. When Lisa foundered in the marketplace because of a high price tag—about $10,000— he made sure GUI appeared in the Macintosh, a trim and stylish new model that he liked to describe as "insanely great."

Jobs was a genuine visionary, but he was also imperious, mercurial, and an erratic manager. When, after an initial year of high sales figures, the Mac encountered some resistance in the marketplace in 1985—compared with the IBM clones it was expensive and had far less available software—Jobs was pushed out of the company. By then Wozniak had left Apple, as well.

IBM, too, had suffered some further jolts, such as the disastrous reception of a toylike home computer called the PCjr in mid-decade. Microsoft, on the other hand, with its lucrative software, was unstoppable. On the day the company went public in 1986, 30-year-old Bill Gates found himself holding stock worth $311 million.

By decade's end, the slick descendants of the humble Altair accounted for about 40 percent of all computer sales, and the growing pervasiveness of personal computers was changing society. A gaggle of magazines had sprung up devoted to the subject *(right, top)*. Children were using computers as naturally as their parents had used pencil and paper. And thanks to miniaturization, almost anyone could afford to wear a computer in the form of a stunningly precise digital wrist watch *(inset)*.

The personal-computer revolution had swept across the nation in less than a decade, and for the front-line participants it had been a wild, exhilarating ride. As a founding member of the Homebrew Computer Club said in fond remembrance, "A year was a lifetime in those days."

Magazines targeting computer users of every kind, from skilled programmers to artists, fed an insatiable appetite for information.

A laser beam scans a bar code, sending a digitized version of the pattern to a computer. By the late '80s, PCs were powerful enough to begin taking over this job from larger machines.

A Machine for All Seasons

By the 1980s processing speed, storage capacity, and other elements of computational prowess had reached a point where the uses of computers almost defied counting. Although the newest computers were nowhere near lifelike, they could, for example, control a robotic hand precisely enough to grip an egg without breaking it *(inset)*. Multi-million-dollar heavyweights such as the Cray X-MP supercomputer could carry out an almost inconceivable 400 million computations per second to forecast the weather or analyze the complicated forces in a nuclear explosion. And even the smallest computers packed a considerable wallop. The first successful portable machine—the Osborne 1, introduced in 1982 by journalist-turned-entrepreneur Adam Osborne—weighed 24 pounds, would fit under an airplane seat, and could run business programs as well as most desktop models.

Osborne foresaw infinite possibilities for computers. "Anything electronic that can happen will happen," he wrote. The growing power of the machines certainly argued for that view. In 1983 *Time* magazine sampled the American scene and found that personal computers were not only embedded in the lives of many stock-

Using a stylus and a wired tablet to control his computer's image-processing software, an FBI artist digitally adds years to a picture of a missing child. Photographs of other members of the family guide him in correctly maturing the lost youngster.

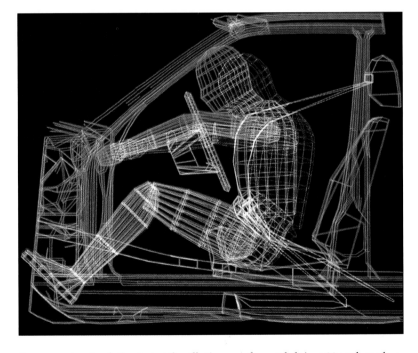

In a computer simulation to test the effectiveness of a seat belt in a 30-mph crash, a human figure slams forward at the instant of impact. Automobile companies were early adopters of computer systems to assist engineers in design and manufacturing.

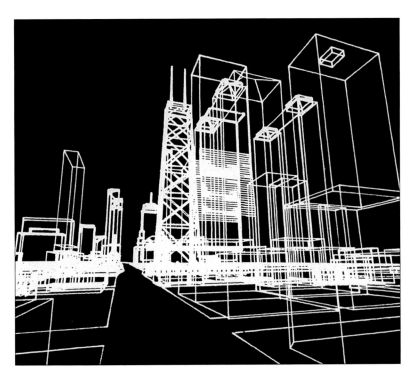

An architectural firm's special hardware and software created these wire-frame drawings of buildings along Chicago's Michigan Avenue. Such drawings depict all of a structure's outlines simultaneously, and the point of view can be altered in an instant.

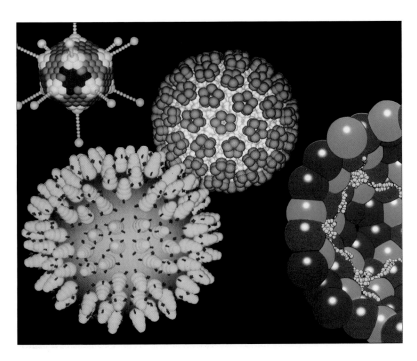

Computer models display the structure of harmful microorganisms in bold colors and sharp detail to aid drug research. Clockwise from upper left: a cold virus, a virus that attacks mice, a virus of tomato plants, and a virus found in mosquitoes.

brokers, storekeepers, salesmen, doctors, lawyers, and other such expected users, but were even making major inroads among such unlikely-seeming customers as farmers. The newsweekly cited the case of Illinois pig farmer Bob Johnson, who used his computer to keep watch over the breeding records of his 300 sows, the yields on 35 test plots of corn, how much feed his hogs ate, and how much the feed cost. "We never had this kind of information before," he said. "It would have taken too long to calculate. But we knew we needed it."

Communication between computers, carried out over phone lines using a signal converter called a modem, expanded their usefulness. That same year, a personal computer could reach into any of 1,450 databases in the U.S. covering everything from airline schedules to movie reviews.

Meanwhile, industry was gaining dramatic efficiencies from computer-related work methods known as CAD/CAM (for Computer-Aided Design/Computer-Aided Manufacturing). Engineers could create on a monitor a precise design for an object— part of a jet engine, say—and then test it under mathematically simulated conditions. The design might then be fed into another computer that controlled machine tools capable of translating it into the real thing.

In a sense, reality itself was being challenged by computers. The mid-1980s saw the first forays into "virtual reality," with voyagers wearing special headsets, gloves, and other gear that could control a software simulation of another world. Instead of looking at a digital realm on a computer's screen, users entered it.

Pac-Man, a chase game based on a voraciously
hungry figure (below) was the hit of the early '80s.

READY!

Electronic Games Take Firm Hold

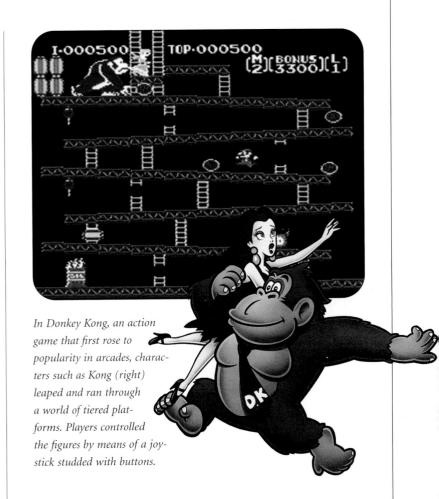

In Donkey Kong, an action game that first rose to popularity in arcades, characters such as Kong (right) leaped and ran through a world of tiered platforms. Players controlled the figures by means of a joystick studded with buttons.

Even as the digital age revolutionized work, it redefined the world's notions of play, with video games leading the way. They burst onto the scene in 1972, when an engineer named Nolan Bushnell founded a company called Atari with a tennis-like arcade game called Pong. By the start of the '80s, Atari and its competitors were offering home systems that hooked up to the TV and played cartridges programmed with a huge variety of games—shoot-'em-ups, chases, martial-arts contests, puzzles, space adventures, and much more. One bestseller was Atari's Pac-Man *(game screen, left)*, featuring a maze, a

Nintendo entertainment system

gobbling mouth, and ghostly pursuers. Another smash hit was Colecovision's 1982 Donkey Kong *(right, top)*.

Video games had their critics. A psychiatrist suggested that they induced a kind of hypnotic trance in children, and the *New England Journal of Medicine* identified a malady called Space Invaders wrist. But the real threats to the video-game industry were oversupply and competition from PCs, which were increasingly used for game playing. Almost overnight, however, the video-game business bounced back. The new leader was Nintendo, which in 1985 offered a sophisticated system *(inset)* and a game called Super Mario Brothers *(right)*—so popular that by decade's end the brothers had their own Saturday cartoon show.

Super Mario Brothers, starring Mario (right) and his twin, Luigi, became the all-time video-game bestseller and helped put Nintendo's hardware in a fifth of all American homes.

Graphic Magic by Computer

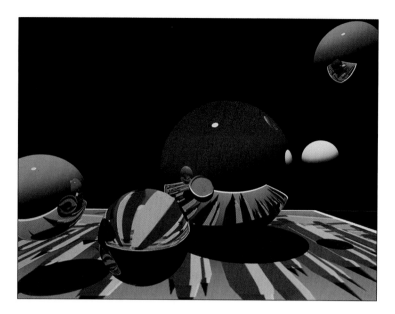

Reflections, refractions, and shadows create a dazzling interplay in a fanciful computer rendition of spheres floating above a palisade of pencils. Five hours of computer time were needed to plot the light paths that make up the image.

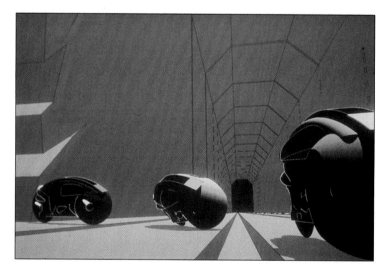

In a scene from the pioneering 1982 movie TRON, digitally created vehicles called lightcycles race through a futuristic world inside a computer. One-third of the full-length film used computer graphics, sometimes melding digital imagery with live action.

Max Headroom (opposite), played by an actor whose voice and features were altered by computer, served as the robotic star of a hit TV show set in a digitally intensive future. The series came to the United States from Great Britain in 1987.

An intriguing new high-tech enterprise of the mid-'80s was a California company called Pixar, founded and overseen—briefly—by the filmmaker George Lucas. In his *Star Wars* epics, Lucas had blazed a trail for computer graphics in movies that Pixar was to advance even further. But Lucas soon sold control to another digital pioneer—Steve Jobs, recently forced out of Apple and looking for a new career.

The field of computer graphics had already come far. For the original *Star Wars* of 1977, Lucas's electronic wizards had spent months doing a computer rendition of the Death Star's innards, but all the work yielded only 90 seconds of screen time. Within a few years, however, faster computers offered a bigger payoff. In 1982, moviegoers were amazed by Disney's *TRON*, a tale of a programming genius sucked into a digital world to do battle with tanks, robots, and other menaces. Modeling the figures and giving surfaces a convincing look required tremendous computing power: A single movie frame might involve calculating values for six million pixels, or picture elements. Of *TRON*'s 30 minutes of computerized film, half was combined with live action and half consisted of footage generated entirely by computer.

As processing speeds grew, the computer-graphics industry found customers in fields as diverse as biochemistry and intelligence gathering. Pixar summed up the trend in an acronymic name it gave to one of its computer systems: REYES, for "Renders Everything You Ever Saw"—and vastly more you couldn't see, as well.

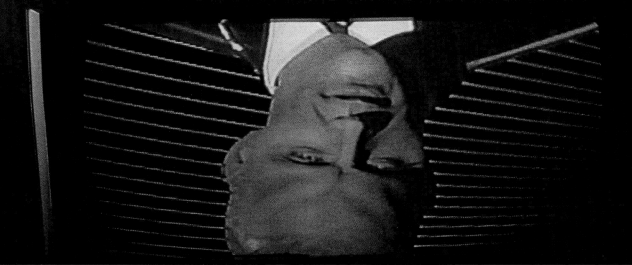

Wall Street's Big Party

★

THE GREED DECADE

I n 1980, the country was in economic misery. Inflation hit 12.5 percent, the worst in 33 years. The prime interest rate reached 21.5 percent, stifling business growth. But the outlook began to change the following year when the new president, Ronald Reagan, cut taxes and social spending while boosting outlays for defense. Reaganomics, as the new policy was dubbed, seemed to work. Interest and inflation rates fell, and millions of new jobs appeared.

For Wall Street, the '80s were one big party. The Dow Jones Industrial Average more than tripled in five years. Young brokers barely out of college bagged six-figure incomes. Companies swallowed up one another at a record pace, often in hostile takeovers. Raiders like Texas oilman T. Boone Pickens *(inset)* reaped big profits even when they *lost* a takeover battle.

But most Americans missed the party. While the wealthiest one-twentieth of families fattened their share of the nation's income by almost 20 percent, the three-fifths at the base of the earnings pyramid saw theirs fall nearly 8 percent. The proportion of children in poverty surged above one-fifth for the first time since the mid-'60s. Hordes of homeless people began haunting city streets.

Wall Street sobered up on October 19, 1987—Black Monday—when the market lost 22.6 percent of its value in the biggest crash on record. The effervescent '80s had lost their fizz.

Twenty minutes before closing time on Black Monday in October 1987, New York Stock Exchange traders frantically seek buyers for their sell orders. The Dow lost a record 508 points.

The Car Guy and The Donald

L ee Iacocca and Donald Trump both became popular business icons of the 1980s, yet they were a study in contrasts. Iacocca was as earthy and personable as Trump was flashy and egotistical. Iacocca rescued Chrysler Corporation from bankruptcy, saving thousands of jobs. Trump parlayed real estate deals into a fortune that enabled him to consume conspicuously. Trump's worth was estimated at between $1 and $3 billion, Iacocca's $20 million.

Iacocca gave both time and money to charity. Trump, too, supported charities, but mainly he acquired trophies, including a 50-room Manhattan penthouse, a 47-room "cottage" in Connecticut, a 118-room Palm Beach mansion, a Boeing 727, and a 282-foot yacht. Iacocca had a home in a Detroit suburb and a condo in Boca Raton.

Each was outspoken in his own way. Iacocca, selling his autos on TV: "If you can find a better car, buy it!" Trump, musing on his life: "I love to have enemies. I like beating my enemies into the ground." And both received relentless media coverage. Trump's fans besieged him for autographs as if he were a movie star; Iacocca's urged him to run for president.

TALKING STRAIGHT
LEE IACOCCA
WITH SONNY KLEINFIELD

Dodge Caravan. A truly revolutionary vehicle. It can handle two adults plus 125 cubic feet of cargo. Or five adults. Even seven with the available rear seat. Yet it's shorter than a full-size station wagon, so it's easier to maneuver and park. And since Caravan stands a mere 5'5", it's easy for you to get in and out of. And it's easy to get Caravan in and out of your garage.

Caravan's 2.2-liter engine rates an est. hwy. of 37 and EPA est. mpg of [24] — impressive mileage for a vehicle of this sort. Caravan also has front-wheel drive to handle slippery surfaces outside and give you more room inside. Yet for all of this, Caravan is remarkably low-priced and even backed by Dodge's 5 year/ 50,000 mile Protection Plan on engine, powertrain and outer body rust-through.

The totally new Dodge Caravan. You've got to see it, sit in it, and drive it to believe it. All of which can happen at your Dodge dealer —where you can buy or lease your very own transportation revolution. Order one now.
The New Chrysler Technology.

INTRODUCING DODGE CARAVAN. A TRANSPORTATION REVOLUTION.

NOT AS LONG AS A FULL-SIZE STATION WAGON, YET IT HOLDS 40% MORE CARGO. AND IT'S ABOUT THE SAME HEIGHT AS THE AVERAGE AMERICAN WOMAN. IT HAS FRONT-WHEEL DRIVE. GETS INCREDIBLE MILEAGE, AND IS BACKED BY 5/50 PROTECTION.

WE ARE DODGE. AN AMERICAN REVOLUTION
Dodge

Lee Iacocca's innovative minivans, like this 1984 Dodge Caravan, helped Chrysler go from $3.1 billion in losses in the late 1970s to a $2.4 billion profit in 1984. His personal successes included Iacocca: An Autobiography, which sold 6.5 million copies, and its popular sequel, Talking Straight (inset).

Trump's wife Ivana—seen below with the man she dubbed The Donald—managed his most prized possession, New York's classic Plaza Hotel. Besides buying numerous Manhattan skyscrapers, Trump also acquired or built several Atlantic City casinos, including the huge, gaudy Taj Mahal, shown in the background.

"I like playing real-life Monopoly."

Donald Trump, 1989

Merger Mania, Junk-Bond Frenzy

The business phenomenon of the 1980s was the merger *(above)*. In the latter half of the decade there were thousands of mergers and buyouts, costing well over one trillion dollars. The fuel for this merger boom? High-yield, high-risk bonds—in common parlance, junk bonds. Traditionally, small companies could not earn bond ratings high enough to tempt investors. To raise money they had to pay high bank interest for short-term loans. But then a few investment houses began underwriting bonds for them. With Wall Street endorsement, these high-interest junk bonds could be sold even to such usually cautious investors as insurance companies and savings and loan associations (S&Ls).

Around this time, Wall Street also was noticing that the true value of some big companies was greater than their total share value. Investment firms began using junk bonds to finance raiders attempting to take over undervalued companies through deals called leveraged buyouts. The winner saddled his prize with the huge debt he had incurred to buy it, then paid the debt off—gradually, from earnings, or quickly, by selling parts of the company.

The original shareholders were usually delighted with the rise in value of their holdings. Employees who lost their jobs, however, were less pleased. So were those who saw peril for the nation in the rapid growth of corporate debt. "Profitable companies are being driven into debt [and] American jobs lost . . . all so that a few enormously wealthy individuals can add to their personal fortunes," said Representative Mary Rose Oakar of Ohio.

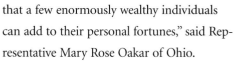

In the biggest merger of the decade, leveraged-buyout specialist Henry Kravis *(opposite, top)* won RJR Nabisco in a particularly fierce battle. Such contests often seemed to owe as much to machismo as to high finance. During the 1989 marriage of Time Inc. and Warner Communications *(inset)*, Paramount Communications boss Martin Davis, like a jealous suitor, tried to step in with an offer to buy Time Inc. Rebuffed, he took his case to court, where he lost.

Eight Largest Takeover Deals Involving U.S. Companies

Buyer	Target	Price ($ bill.)	Year
Kohlberg Kravis Roberts	RJR Nabisco	25.1	1988
Standard Oil of California	Gulf Oil	13.2	1984
Philip Morris	Kraft	13.1	1988
Bristol-Myers	Squibb	12.0	1989
Time Inc.	Warner Com.	11.7	1989
British Petroleum	Standard Oil	7.9	1987
SmithKline Beckman	Beecham	7.9	1989
Du Pont	Conoco	7.6	1981

Actor Michael Douglas (inset) as Gordon Gekko in Wall Street—the 1987 hit movie about runaway greed—mimes real-life takeover tycoon Henry Kravis (top), although his character more closely resembled crooked stock trader Ivan Boesky (page 95). Kravis projects the calm, cold power described in Barbarians at the Gate, a book about the RJR Nabisco merger battle: "There was a steely glint in his eyes that made one want to believe the stories of unbridled greed and ambition."

Greed Taken to Felonious Extremes

In mid-1985 investigators for the Securities and Exchange Commission (SEC) learned that suspicious stock trades were being made for an account in a Swiss bank's Bahamas branch. After a year of digging they identified the account holder. It was the first step in uncovering what *Time* magazine called "the worst insider trading scandal in U.S. history."

The account belonged to one Dennis Levine, managing director of Drexel Burnham Lambert, the brokerage firm that pioneered the use of junk bonds in corporate takeovers. Levine used the account to secretly buy shares in companies he knew were targeted for takeovers—before public knowledge pushed the prices up. In a deal with prosecutors, Levine told how he had sold insider information to Ivan Boesky, famous on Wall Street as Ivan the Terrible, an arbitrageur who bought and sold stock in companies involved in, or threatened with, takeovers. Boesky had paid Levine $2.4 million for the tips. To save what he could of his own skin, Boesky in turn gave up the biggest shark of all: Michael Milken.

Milken, head of Drexel Burnham Lambert's junk-bond division, had virtually invented the way the bonds were used in takeover wars and had made himself and his firm unimaginably rich in the process. His personal wealth was estimated at more than a billion dollars. According to investigators, however, much of that wealth came as a result of insider trading, fraud, stock manipulation, and other securities violations. As the whole sordid mess unfolded, one academic observer sighed, "Where we're at today is really no different from the age of the robber barons."

In 1988 Drexel Burnham Lambert pleaded guilty to six felonies and agreed to pay $650 million in fines. Milken was indicted on 98 counts. Like the other defendants, he agreed to a plea bargain. He drew a 10-year prison sentence, later reduced to three, and paid the largest fine ever levied on an individual, $600 million. Boesky served two years in prison and coughed up $100 million. Levine got 17 months, had to return $11.6 million in profits, and was fined $300,000. All three were barred from securities work for life.

Michael Milken, whom Time called "the presiding financial genius of the Roaring Eighties," swears to tell the truth at a 1988 SEC hearing. A professor of business ethics said his conviction "punctuates the end of an era of greed, excess, and money madness."

Ivan Boesky poses for a mug shot after being arrested in 1987. Investigators showed that insider knowledge had guided his sure-bet investments and garnered him $200 million. "I am deeply ashamed," he told the judge. "I have spent the last year trying to understand how I veered off course."

> "Greed is not a bad thing. Everybody should be a little greedy. . . . You shouldn't feel guilty."

Ivan Boesky, 1985

Black Monday

On a Friday, a 4.5 percent drop in the Dow touched off a tremor that was felt around the world. Three days later, amplified by slumping markets in Asia and Europe, it slammed back into Wall Street on Monday, October 19, 1987, as a quake of epic dimensions. Total share values fell half a trillion dollars—an amount equal to the gross national product of France.

The crash, which left the market 36 percent below its August peak, was blamed on a huge U.S. trade deficit, big federal budget deficits, the threat of renewed inflation and higher interest rates, and new-fangled computerized program trading. Some observers also noted that, just as in 1929, this big crash was preceded by revelations about Wall Street insiders cheating the public, a scandal that was certain to have undermined investor confidence.

The Dow recovered its losses before the end of 1989 and was pushing toward new highs, but the investment

A New York Stock Exchange broker cradles his head, exhausted by Black Monday's torrent of orders. More than 600 million shares were traded, almost

industry did not fare so well. Junk-bond prices fell by half or more, partly because many of their issuers were defaulting and partly because a new law forced S&Ls to rid their investment portfolios of junk. The pace of takeovers inevitably slowed, and many investment houses were hurt.

Before the decade ended, some 37,000 Wall Street employees had been laid off. The go-go investment powerhouse Drexel Burnham Lambert was lurching toward bankruptcy, which would soon throw 5,300 more employees out of work. The party was definitely over.

"This is going to make 1929 look like a kiddie party."

Los Angeles stock trader, October 19, 1987

double the previous record. At day's end the ticker was two hours behind.

A reader on Wall Street gets the Black Monday news from a New York Post special edition. Across America crowds formed outside brokers' offices to follow plunging prices on electronic tickers or television monitors. In Boston, police asked a brokerage firm to switch off its ticker because anxious investors were blocking the street.

A New Galaxy
of Superstars

★

BIG WINS, BIG LOSSES, BIG BUCKS

Still reeling from a 10-3 blowout at the hands of the Soviet hockey team just a week before the 1980 Olympics, U.S. coach Herb Brooks was more hopeful than confident as the February 22 semifinal with the Soviets approached. "Coach, you just wait," said Jim Craig, his goalie. "You haven't seen it yet."

"It" turned out to be a virtuoso example of team play, and the nation held its breath as TV announcer Al Michaels counted down the final seconds. "Do you believe in miracles?" he shouted. "Yes!" Final score: U.S. 4, Soviet Union 3. Two days later the Americans beat Finland 4-2, winning the gold medal to the cry "USA! USA! USA!"

The hockey team's "Miracle on Ice" ushered in a decade of awesome performances by an array of gifted athletes, including Michael Jordan *(inset)*, who began his pro career in 1985 by being named Rookie of the Year. These stars, hyped by relentless television coverage, lifted college games, the pros, and the Olympics to new heights—economic as well as athletic. By 1987, the total value of goods and services produced by sports in the United States was estimated at $50.2 billion—1.1 percent of the nation's gross national product. Ironically, amid this sea of plenty, the sporting world managed to sully itself with scandal, drug abuse, and labor disputes. Yet on balance, the 1980s were a time of stellar athletic achievement.

Michael Jordan

The U.S. hockey team explodes with jubilation as the buzzer seals their upset victory over the Soviets at the 1980 Winter Games. Fifteen of the Americans went on to play in the National Hockey League.

Olympic Dreams— Not All Came True

On his first long jump in the 1984 Olympics, Carl Lewis soars 28' ¼", far enough to win. Confident about that jump and nursing some soreness, Lewis made only one other leap of the six allowed.

"My job is just to compete as an athlete and be a nice guy. Jesse Owens is still the same to me, a legend. I'm just a person with some God-given talent."

Carl Lewis, on duplicating Jesse Owens's 1936 four-gold-medal performance

Almost lost in the euphoria of the U.S. hockey team's win at Lake Placid was Eric Heiden's incredible speed-skating performance. Not only did Heiden win five gold medals, but he did so at every distance from 500 meters to 10,000—an unheard-of exhibit of athletic versatility—and he broke a record in each race. Said a Norwegian skating coach, "We have no idea how to train to take him. We just hope he retires."

The United States boycotted the 1980 Summer Games in Moscow after the Soviet Union invaded Afghanistan. In retaliation, the U.S.S.R. and its Eastern Bloc allies stayed home when Los Angeles hosted the 1984 Olympiad. Against the somewhat diluted competition offered up by 7,458 athletes from 139 countries, the Americans won a record 83 golds, more than the combined gold, silver, and bronze count of any other nation.

Among the brightest stars was Carl Lewis (left), who, like Jesse Owens in 1936, won the 100 meters, 200 meters, long jump, and 4 x 100-meter relay. Greg Louganis (right) displayed versatility as well, becoming the first man in 56 years to capture gold for both the springboard and the 10-meter platform diving events. Gymnast Mary Lou Retton (page 102), an ebullient 4'9" 16-year-old, won four medals, including top prize in the all-around competition—the first individual gymnastic medal ever won by an American. Of her perfect, medal-clinching vault she said, "I *knew* I had it. I knew it when I was in the *air!*"

With a full roster of competitors at the 1988 Summer Games in Seoul, South Korea, the United States took fewer gold medals than four years earlier, but many American athletes still performed spectacularly. Swimmer Matt Biondi won five golds, a silver, and a bronze. Janet Evans added three swimming golds to the U.S. tally, and Louganis repeated his wins in the diving events—despite being

Greg Louganis displays the form that won him two golds each at the 1984 and 1988 Olympics. Asked to explain his style, he said, "Diving should be like poetry. It should always be flowing."

briefly put off his game when he struck his head on the springboard during a dive. The flamboyant Florence Griffith-Joyner, known as FloJo (*opposite*), blazed to victory in the 100 meters, 200 meters, and 4 x 100-meter relay and won a silver with the 4 x 400-meter relay team.

Not all of America's premier athletes realized their Olympic dreams. Mary Decker, the nation's top female middle-distance runner, was finally competing in an Olympics after many disappointments. She was squared off in the 3,000 meters against a field that included barefoot runner Zola Budd, a South African who had hastily adopted British citizenship to get around the Olympic embargo against her homeland. Midway through the race Decker got tangled up with Budd and fell hard, losing her best chance at Olympic gold. And the 1988 basketball team, featuring future NBA stars David Robinson, Mitch Richmond, and Danny Manning, lost to the Soviets 82-76.

Sprinter Florence Griffith-Joyner (right) exults after streaking to victory in the 100-meter dash in Seoul. Because of a tailwind, her run of 10.54 seconds did not count as an Olympic record for the 100, but her 200-meter time stood as a new world record.

Gymnast Mary Lou Retton nails her climactic vault—a layout back somersault with a double twist—at the 1984 Olympic Games. The irrepressible West Virginian's perfect 10 enabled her to overhaul a tough Rumanian rival to win the women's all-around gold by five-hundredths of a point.

New Records and 49ers Football

Joe Montana saved his best performances for the biggest games. With his 49ers trailing the Cincinnati Bengals 16-13 and only three minutes to play in the 1989 Super Bowl, he orchestrated a 92-yard drive for the winning touchdown. The league's most accurate passer ever, Montana never threw an interception in a Super Bowl.

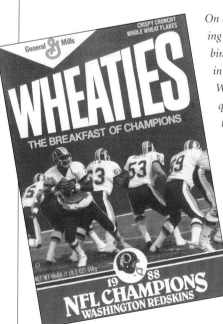

On a cereal box commemorating the Redskins' 42-10 drubbing of the Denver Broncos in Super Bowl XXII, Doug Williams, the first black quarterback in the history of the championship, drops back to pass behind his immense offensive line, nicknamed the Hogs. Washington played in three Super Bowls during the decade, winning two.

As an icon of 1980s pro football, nothing could surpass the sight of Chicago Bears running back Walter Payton eluding outmaneuvered, frozen defenders *(right)*. Said Washington Redskins defensive tackle Darryl Grant, "Maybe there was some other guy, who is now unknown to man, who carried a stone for more yards. But as far as we know, Payton's the greatest." By the time he retired, in 1987, he had run for 16,726 yards, eclipsing Jim Brown's 19-year-old career rushing mark.

When it came to setting records, Payton had company. In 1983 Redskins runner John Riggins broke O. J. Simpson's season record for touchdowns with 24. The next year Eric Dickerson of the Los Angeles Rams ran for 2,105 yards, burying another Simpson mark. The decade also saw the debut of such future Hall of Famers as quarterbacks Dan Marino of the Miami Dolphins, John Elway of the Denver Broncos, and Jim Kelly of the Buffalo Bills, as well as New York Giants linebacker Lawrence Taylor.

The San Francisco 49ers were the team of the '80s. Deploying an offense based on short passes and quick thinking, they were all but unstoppable. With quarterback Joe Montana *(above, left)* passing to ace receiver Jerry Rice—who could "catch a BB in the dark," said one coach—the 49ers enjoyed four Super Bowl championship seasons.

The National Football League (NFL) remained popular despite player strikes in 1982 and 1987—when replacement players substituted for the regulars in four games—and the moves of three teams to new cities. Television revenues were greater than ever, and several teams broke ground for new stadiums to hold ever increasing crowds.

Chicago's Walter Payton, hurdling a tackler at right, gained 100 yards or more in 77 games and had ten 1,000-yard seasons, both NFL records. In 1986 he finally won a Super Bowl ring.

The Bird and Magic Show

In the late 1970s the National Basketball Association was in trouble, with several franchises facing bankruptcy. But the 1979-80 season introduced two charismatic rookies—Earvin "Magic" Johnson *(opposite)* of the Los Angeles Lakers and Larry Bird *(below)* of the Boston Celtics—who launched a renaissance that helped turn the league into a billion-dollar enterprise. As the decade progressed, the NBA would showcase many all-time greats—Kareem Abdul Jabbar, Julius Erving, and Moses Malone, as well as newcomers Michael Jordan, Hakeem Olajuwon, Charles Barkley, John Stockton, Karl Malone,

and Isiah Thomas. But Bird and Magic outshone them all.

The same height (6'9") and weight (220 pounds), the two superstars shared a passion for the game, a dedication to fundamentals, and a relentless will to win. Yet they also symbolized opposites—one was white, the other black; one was East Coast grit, the other West Coast glitz; one was a smooth-shooting forward, the other a flashy point guard. "I only know how to play two ways," said Magic, mangling an expression. "That's reckless and abandon."

During the '80s Magic's Lakers won five NBA titles, Bird's Celtics three. Three times the men met in the finals (1984, '85, and '87), with the Lakers prevailing twice. Each won the NBA's Most Valuable Player award three times, and each liked and respected the other. Magic of Bird: "He was the only player that I truly feared." Said Bird, "Magic is a great, great basketball player. The best I've ever seen."

Larry Bird scores on a twisting left-handed lay-up. In his rookie year, the self-styled Hick from French Lick, Indiana, led the Celtics to 61 wins, 32 more than the previous year—the greatest turnaround in NBA history. Explaining his approach to the game, Bird said, "The number one thing is desire."

Magic Johnson runs the Lakers' famous "Showtime" attack in the celebrity-packed Los Angeles Forum. Julius Erving called him "the only player who could take only three shots and still dominate a game." In the deciding contest of the 1980 finals against Philadelphia, the versatile Johnson played all five positions.

Edmonton's Wayne Gretzky (99), a
phenomenon on ice, carries the puck
toward the Islanders' net during the
1983 Stanley Cup finals.

Two Dynasties Face Off

As far as I'm concerned," boasted Denis Potvin, captain of the New York Islanders in 1983, "we're the best hockey team ever to lace on skates." If Potvin exaggerated, it was not by much. His team had just won its fourth Stanley Cup in a row, a feat exceeded only by the 1956-60 Montreal Canadiens.

The Islanders' victims in their fourth championship year were the Edmonton Oilers, who not only lost the Cup but were swept four games to zero. But the Oilers came back to get their first Stanley Cup a year later—and did it again in 1985, '87, and '88, ending the Islanders' dynasty and establishing their own.

The Oilers' style of play was perfectly suited to center Wayne Gretzky *(left)*. First called the Great One during his peewee-league days, Gretzky rewrote the record book. In the 1980-81 season, his second in the NHL, Gretzky amassed 164 points, the most ever, on 55 goals and 109 assists. The following year, he upped his record to 212 points, including an all-time high of 92 goals. In October 1989, he surpassed Gordie Howe's NHL career mark of 1,850 points. Gretzky also set career Stanley Cup playoff records for goals, assists, and points, and he won the Hart Memorial Trophy, the league's Most Valuable Player award, nine times in his first 10 years. "If you want to tell me he's the greatest player of all time," said Howe, "I have no argument at all."

In 1989, at the ripe old baseball age of 42, Nolan Ryan struck out 301 batters in 239 ⅓ innings and won 16 games. Opposing batters hit a mere .187 against him.

A Decade of Big Hits— and Foul Balls

The 1980s found major-league baseball in a struggle to keep fans' attention on the action in the ballparks. Two player strikes, costing one-third of the season in 1981 and two days in 1985, were garnished with drug, alcohol, and gambling scandals. Even nature seemed to bear a grudge: An earthquake in California delayed the start of the 1989 World Series for 10 days *(pages 128-129)*.

Memorable moments helped to compensate. In game six of the 1986 World Series, the Boston Red Sox were one out away from their first championship in 68 years. But the New York Mets rallied to win after Red Sox first baseman Bill Buckner, hobbled with injuries, let a routine grounder go through his legs. In the seventh game, the Red Sox took a 3-0 lead into the sixth inning, only to lose the game 8-5, and along with it the Series.

Several longstanding records fell. In 1985, Pete Rose collected hit number 4,192, topping Ty Cobb's career mark. "A hundred years from now,"

Ricky Henderson of the Oakland Athletics sprints for second base and slides in headfirst, beating the tag of Milwaukee shortstop Robin Yount to break Lou Brock's season record of 118 stolen bases on August 27, 1982. Below, the 23-year-old outfielder lifts the base in salute to Brock, on hand for the occasion. Henderson finished the year with 130 steals. Strangely, he was also tagged out 42 times attempting to steal, topping the record of 38 set by Ty Cobb.

predicted Rose, unconcerned with the reaction to his compulsion to break Cobb's record, "people will just remember me as the guy with the most hits." Events, though, would take a different turn *(overleaf)*.

Nolan Ryan *(opposite, below)* obliterated Walter Johnson's career strikeout record of 3,508 and threw his fifth no-hitter—one more than Sandy Koufax's career record—to keep the Houston Astros ahead of the Cincinnati Reds in the 1981 race for the National League pennant. "This was the best," said Ryan later, "not just because it sets the record, but because it was a big game and my mom was here to see it. It's the first one of my no-hitters she's seen."

A new face, 23-year-old Ricky Henderson *(above)*, broke the season record for stolen bases. Roger Clemens struck out 20 batters in a single game. And pitcher Orel Hershiser set a new standard for consecutive scoreless innings with 59. In 1985 Dwight Gooden enjoyed one of the best seasons of any pitcher, leading the National League in wins (24), earned-run average (1.53), and strikeouts (268). Wade Boggs and Tony Gwynn won nine batting titles between them. But the top hitter was George Brett of the Kansas City Royals. In 1980 he hit .390, the highest average since Ted Williams's .406 in 1941.

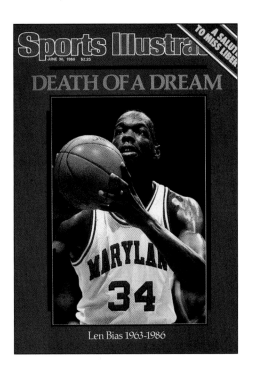

Len Bias's death from cocaine stunned the nation. By all accounts, the drug killed him the first time he tried it.

A sure Hall of Fame spot eluded Pete Rose when he was banned from baseball for life in 1989 for betting on his own team.

Black Eyes for Big-Time Sports

Sports stars' human failings were an unhappy hallmark of the decade. The bad tidings began with the worst case of corruption in collegiate athletics since the basketball point-shaving scandals of 1950. For falsifying players' academic records, five schools in the Pacific-10 Conference were declared ineligible for the 1980 league championship and postseason bowl games. The National Collegiate Athletic Association punished other schools for breaking recruiting regulations. Violations were so outrageous at Southern Methodist University that the 1987 football team received the so-called death penalty; its season was canceled.

Worse news came from professional sports. In 1982, reports of players high on drugs or alcohol rocked the NFL. Substance abuse also infected baseball. In 1984, four members of the Kansas City Royals went to prison for possessing or trying to buy cocaine. The following year, Keith Hernandez of the New York Mets testified that 40 percent of big-league players had sampled the drug. One, as it turned out, was Hernandez's teammate Dwight Gooden, who entered a treatment program in 1987.

The 1988 Summer Olympics were besmirched by 10 athletes—among them world champion sprinter Ben Johnson of Canada *(right)*—who tested positive for performance-enhancing substances. After winning the 100-meter dash in a best-ever 9.79 seconds, Johnson told reporters, "This record will last 50 years, maybe 100." It lasted three days, the time it took Olympic officials to test and retest Johnson's urine, strip him of his gold medal, and bar him from racing for two years—later extended to a lifetime ban. "I think it's wonderful," Mary Decker Slaney said of the decision. "Not because of Ben, but because I want a clean sport."

The most tragic sports news of the decade hit on June 19, 1986, when 22-year-old basketball star Len Bias *(top left)*, the 6'8" All-American forward from the University of Maryland, died of a cocaine-induced heart attack. Two days earlier Bias had been selected as the Boston Celtics' top draft pick. Said the Celtics' Larry Bird, "It's the cruelest thing I've ever heard."

Canada's Ben Johnson bursts ahead of the pack to win the 100-meter dash at the 1988 Olympics. A few days later, having found traces of anabolic steroids in his urine, Olympic officials gave his gold medal to archrival Carl Lewis.

A Lineup of Champions

Classic rivalries made for great golf and tennis, beginning with the 1980 Wimbledon final. Sweden's Bjorn Borg beat American John McEnroe to win his fifth straight championship. The next year, however, McEnroe *(below)* bested Borg to begin several years atop the ranks of men's tennis. Martina Navratilova *(right)* became virtually unbeatable in the women's game.

In golf, Tom Watson *(opposite, bottom)* snatched a major tournament from Jack Nicklaus and ended up a three-time Professional Golfers' Association Player of the Year. In 1986, Greg LeMond became the first American to win the Tour de France and won again in 1989 *(opposite, top)*.

Queen of the Courts

Arguably the best female player ever, Martina Navratilova dominated women's tennis with her attacking style, set up by a powerful left-handed serve (above). In 1982 and '83 her record was a phenomenal 176-4. She won 15 Grand Slam singles titles during the decade, including six straight Wimbledons and four U.S. Opens. "If I'm on," she said, "nobody can beat me."

Contentious Conqueror

John McEnroe celebrates his 1981 defeat of Bjorn Borg in the finals at Wimbledon, ending Borg's five-year unbroken run of 41 victories. A left-hander with a light touch but a bad temper, McEnroe won two more Wimbledons, four U.S. Opens, and 10 Grand Slam doubles championships. He was ranked number one among men tennis players from 1981 to 1984, a year when he compiled an 82-3 record.

Greyhound on Wheels

Straining every sinew, Greg LeMond sprints for the finish on the last day of the 1989 Tour de France. He began the 24.5-kilometer time trial trailing Laurent Fignon of France by a seemingly insurmountable 50 seconds. LeMond's time of 26:57 gave him the win by eight seconds. Said America's greatest cyclist after the victory, "I never stopped believing I could do it."

A Shot for the Ages

Standing on a down slope facing a slick green on the 17th hole at Pebble Beach, Tom Watson chips in for a birdie in the 1982 U.S. Open. Called "a thousand-to-one shot" by runner-up Jack Nicklaus, the 16-footer led to Watson's first U.S. Open victory. But it was no fluke. "I've practiced that shot," said Watson, "for hours, days, months, and years."

Twenty-year-old Mike Tyson hammers Trevor Berbick in their 1986 title bout. Tyson scored a second-round technical knockout to become the youngest heavyweight champion ever.

Iron Mike and Sugar Ray

Deep inside Iron Mike Tyson dwelt a primal force. Unleashed in the ring *(left)*, it was devastating. Tyson, who had spent most of his youth in juvenile detention centers, began boxing in 1980 at age 13 under 72-year-old trainer Cus D'Amato. Before the decade was out, he won 36 straight fights, all but four by knockouts. In 1987, he captured all three heavy-weight titles—those of the World Boxing Council, the World Boxing Association, and the International Boxing Federation.

Tyson was perhaps the most bruising of the fighters who revived interest in the sport in the '80s. But none had more fans than his contemporary near the lighter end of boxing's weight classes, Sugar Ray Leonard, a master boxer with a powerful punch. By decade's end, he had fought his way to a 36-1-1 record, world championships at three different weights, and more than $100 million in prize money. His only defeat came in June 1980 in a close decision favoring former lightweight champion Roberto Duran. Leonard not only avenged that loss twice but also defeated the unbeaten Tommy "Hit Man" Hearns and, after retiring twice, came back in 1987 to defeat the World Boxing Council middleweight champion, "Marvelous" Marvin Hagler *(inset)*.

Trials of the Human Spirit

★

THE DECADE'S BIGGEST HEADLINES

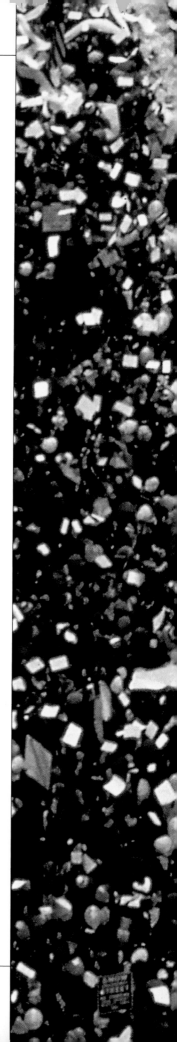

For more than 14 months the nation had endured humiliation. But now, on January 20, 1981, it was finally over. Fifty-two Americans, taken hostage when Iranian mobs stormed the U.S. embassy in Tehran—were coming home. After scornfully brushing off ineffectual threats and offers to negotiate from the Carter administration, the Iranians had suddenly seen fit to cut a deal. They were, after all, confronting a new and perhaps tougher American president, and pressure was mounting in their savage war against neighboring Iraq.

In return for the hostages, the United States released an initial $2.8 billion of about $12 billion in frozen Iranian assets. That seemed a small enough price as an overjoyed America greeted the hostage-heroes with pealing church bells and blizzards of confetti (right). Despite having suffered brutal treatment, the hostages were a tough bunch and swiftly set about rebuilding their lives. Restoring U.S. prestige would take longer.

Nevertheless, it was a bright start to a decade whose headlines all too often reflected tragedy, want, ecological disaster, and nature's revenge. Yet for all that, there were further reasons to cheer, notably in the triumph of the human spirit over two symbols of bleakest oppression: South African apartheid and the Berlin Wall.

A New York City ticker-tape parade (right), that grand old custom, welcomes hostages back from Iran. Above, assistant U.S. Air Force attaché David Roeder lets go a cheer after his first breath of free air.

Tragic First—A Fatal Space Mission

Led by flight commander Francis "Dick" Scobee, the Challenger crew—from front to rear, electrical engineer Judith Resnik, physicist Ronald McNair, pilot Michael Smith, high-school teacher Christa McAuliffe, aerospace engineer Ellison Onizuka, and electrical engineer Gregory Jarvis—head for launch complex 39-B.

With the whole world watching—including a gathering of stunned students at Christa McAuliffe's high school in Concord, New Hampshire—the Challenger explodes, producing the hauntingly eerie sight of a fireball and arcs of smoke.

"R outine" was the word for U.S. manned space flights. By January 1986 Americans had rocketed aloft 55 times with such success that their safe return was taken for granted—all the more so because for the past five years astronauts had been practically commuting to their work in space aboard four flawlessly performing shuttles. So confident was NASA that even nonprofessionals were being invited to go up: a senator, a congressman, a Saudi prince. Better still, symbolizing what seemed to be the imminent new era of space travel for everyman, the first ordinary citizen would be shot into orbit. She was Christa McAuliffe, 37, mother of two, a Concord, New Hampshire, social studies teacher, who on closed-circuit TV would show millions of kids how wonderfully easy it all was.

Mission 51-L, the 25th shuttle flight, had objectives besides taking Christa McAuliffe on what was called "the ultimate field trip." The pilot, copilot, and four mission specialists would put a $100 million communications satellite into orbit and conduct various ultraviolet-ray, radiation, and weightlessness experiments. Like McAuliffe, they were "rarin' to go"—especially after delays had pushed the flight back eight days to January 28.

Liftoff at Cape Canaveral was perfect, the *Challenger* thundering up, up, up. But then, 73 seconds into the flight, tracking cameras witnessed a glow of light between the shuttle and its external fuel tank. Milliseconds later, *Challenger* disintegrated in a monstrous blossom of orange flame. A booster rocket had failed, igniting the tank and sending Christa McAuliffe and her comrades to their doom.

The unbearable, the secret dread had been realized. In one fiery instant, the bubble of complacency about manned space flight had burst. No shuttle would fly again until 1988. "We all knew it could happen one day," said a rocket scientist, "but God, who would have believed it?"

"They slipped the surly bonds of Earth to touch the face of God."

President Ronald Reagan, 1986

> "If you stay in this business long enough, it'll get you."

John Lennon, 1978, after Elvis Presley's death

A chance snapshot shows John Lennon signing one of his albums for a demented Mark Chapman, who would shoot him dead a few hours later. Opposite, flowers, candles, and a poignant photo testify to the many memorial vigils fans held for Lennon.

Grief Comes to a Generation

Mr. Lennon." John Lennon was turning toward the voice when four .38-cal. bullets ripped into his body. The beloved former Beatle staggered across the courtyard of his New York apartment building and fell dead. It was December 8, 1980. He was 40 years old. Lennon's killer was Mark David Chapman, a 25-year-old Hawaii resident with a history of mental problems. Formerly a fan, Chapman had persuaded himself that his one-time hero was now a money-hungry sellout.

The violent death of a man who had devoted his musical gifts to the cause of peace shocked the world. An entire generation wept, for Lennon's passing shattered one of their most fervent dreams—that he, Paul McCartney, George Harrison, and Ringo Starr would "Come Together" again, and the hopeful world the Beatles had once personified would somehow be put back on its tracks.

In 1966 Lennon had met Yoko Ono, a Japanese avant-garde artist. Her presence sowed dissension between Lennon and the other Beatles, and in 1969, after he and Yoko wed, Lennon told Paul, George, and Ringo that he wanted out of the group.

Following the Beatles' breakup Lennon and Yoko moved to New York, where he became an active peace advocate, winning new fans and admirers with his anti-Vietnam War efforts and with such prayerful anthems as "Imagine" and "Give Peace a Chance." He also won the enmity of the Nixon administration, which sought to kick him out of the country.

In 1973 he and Yoko split up, a separation that lasted for two years, during which Lennon not only fought deportation—"It just seemed like a toothache that wouldn't go away"—but also struggled with substance abuse. Things got better after the couple reconciled. In October 1975 they had a son, Sean. Lennon cared for the baby while Yoko managed their holdings, totaling over $200 million. And in 1976 the toothache finally went away; he was granted a "green card"—resident alien status.

Throughout his post-Beatles decade this rock genius had continued to make music; the album *Double Fantasy* (November 1980) was the last work released before his death. Later there would be still more of Lennon's music, but it all would be tinged with a sense of irreparable loss.

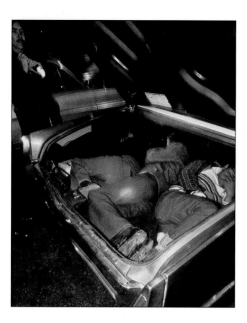

An officer shines his light into a car trunk jammed with foreigners trying to slip into the U.S. near San Diego in 1981. An estimated 3,000 Mexicans made the attempt in this area every night.

"Regardless of what country you come from, one still sees America . . . as dreamland, where you can be what you want to be."

Demetre Belgis, Greek immigrant, 1985

Opposite, a gallery of immigrants speaks to the enormous diversity brought forth by the abolition of the old biased quota system. By 1990, one out of every 12 Americans had been born somewhere else.

In Search of a Better Life

They came from the ends of the earth and all points in between, the greatest surge of immigrants since the early 1900s. In 1984 alone 544,000 legal immigrants arrived. But where earlier waves had sailed across the Atlantic from the Old World, these new immigrants came mostly from the Third World, notably Hispanic America and Asia.

Far greater still—and more troubling to many Americans—was a tidal wave of illegal immigrants, mainly Mexicans pouring across the 2,000-mile southern border. The U.S. Border Patrol stopped 1.3 million illegals in 1984 but estimated that several times that number evaded its vigilance.

The main reason for the upsurge in legal immigration was an end in 1965 to a system that had long favored Western and northern Europeans. Now America beckoned to everyone, and the newcomers, legal and illegal, were changing the face of the country, from its racial makeup to its tastes in food, clothing, and music. There was a Little Havana in Miami, a Little Saigon in California's Orange County, a Koreatown in Los Angeles. In fact, the Los Angeles County court system provided interpreters for 80 different languages.

As Americans struggled with the staggering statistic that fully two-thirds of the entire world's immigration was focused on the United States, they were asking themselves, How many people of how many races, colors, creeds, and languages could the country assimilate? How much unskilled labor did this high-tech society need? Were the newcomers grabbing jobs from our native-born poor and disadvantaged blacks?

In a 1985 *Time* magazine poll, two-thirds of those surveyed said that the United States should strictly limit immigration, and 75 percent demanded a crackdown on illegal aliens. Yet two-thirds also agreed that the newcomers made productive citizens once they were established.

So it might be that the United States could not assimilate everybody in the old melting-pot sense, that the *Pluribus* in the American slogan *E Pluribus Unum* ("one out of many") would gain ground on the *Unum*. But was that so bad? Had there ever really been a melting pot, anyway? Besides, as Lam Ton, a Vietnamese restaurateur in Chicago put the case for the many immigrants who were refugees: "This is the last stand. There is nowhere else to run."

Ghana

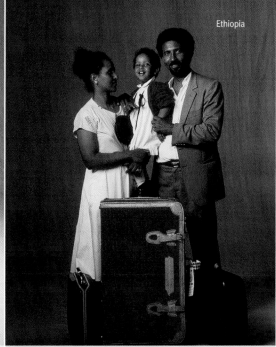

Ethiopia

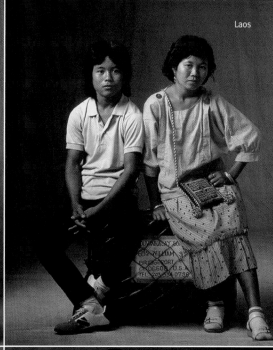

Laos

Soviet Union

Cambodia

India

Philippines

Afghanistan

South Korea

A Plague of Loss and Grief

The first hint of a problem came from Los Angeles. On June 5, 1981, a physician advised the federal Centers for Disease Control (CDC) that he had just treated five young homosexual males for a rare type of pneumonia. By August the CDC had received more than 100 such reports, now on both coasts and involving a dozen diseases.

No one realized it yet, but the awful scourge that would soon be labeled AIDS—acquired immune deficiency syndrome—had arrived. In 1983 scientists discovered that the deadly new malady was caused by something called the human immunodeficiency virus (HIV). The virus was transmitted through unprotected sex or other fluid exchange, and it rendered the

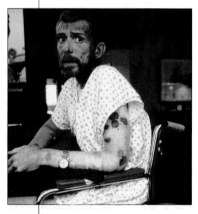

body's immune system helpless against other diseases. HIV had originated in Africa, eventually reached the United States, and was now running rampant, particularly among gay men.

The initial political and public reaction to this apparent "gay plague" was one of widespread indifference, or even grim satisfaction. Then Hollywood he-man Rock Hudson, 59, announced that he was a homosexual who had AIDS. The news jolted the national consciousness. The epidemic had also reached heterosexuals. It began among needle-sharing drug addicts and prostitutes and spread to their customers, lovers, wives, and children. When some cases were traced to blood transfusions, the public's sense of being safely distant from the threat was shattered.

"Safe sex" education dramatically reduced the incidence of AIDS among homosexuals, but the overall rates of HIV infection kept climbing until by May 1989 nearly 100,000 cases of AIDS had been diagnosed, with 56,468 deaths. A few drugs of very limited effectiveness appeared, but there was nothing else. The terrible death toll just kept accelerating. "The word *cure*," said one immunologist, "is not yet in the vocabulary."

Looking wan and haunted shortly before his death at age 45 in 1986, gay activist and AIDS sufferer Ken Meeks (above) displays the lesions of Kaposi's sarcoma, a rare skin cancer previously found mostly in the elderly but often associated with the new disease.

A patchwork quilt with the names of thousands of AIDS victims is spread out on the Washington Mall in October 1987. Part of an AIDS fund-raising project, the quilt was a way for family and friends of the dead to comfort one another.

Two cars lie at drunken angles where the upper roadway of the Bay Bridge, linking San Francisco and Oakland, collapsed onto the lower level. A motorcyclist described the scene as "like bumper cars—only you could die in this game."

Fifteen Seconds
of Devastation

Nothing like it had rocked the United States since the Alaska quake of 1964. It was 5:04 on the afternoon of October 17, 1989, and millions of Americans were settling down to watch the opening game of the first World Series ever to be played entirely in the San Francisco Bay area—the San Francisco Giants vs. the Oakland Athletics. Suddenly the earth started heaving and buckling with a roar like thunder, and the telecast from the Giants' Candlestick Park was abruptly cut off. Though the tremor measured a fearsome 7.1 on the Richter scale, it lasted just 15 seconds. But that was quite enough.

People were hurled to the ground; buildings dissolved into dust; gas lines ruptured and burst into flame. The epicenter lay 75 miles south, but the worst damage occurred in the Bay area. Rush-hour drivers on the Bay Bridge froze in horror as a 50-foot section of upper deck toppled onto the lower roadway, slamming cars into one another *(left)*. In West Oakland a mile-long section of the double-decked I-880 freeway pancaked onto the lower roadway, crushing vehicles and killing 42 people.

The final toll was 67 dead, more than 3,000 injured, 14,000 homeless, and $10 billion in damage. Seismologists warned that Californians faced a 50-50 chance of a similar quake happening sometime in the next 30 years.

A house awaits demolition in the Marina section of San Francisco. The neighborhood was particularly hard hit because it was built on soft fill reclaimed from the bay.

South Africa's best-known churchman, Anglican archbishop Desmond Tutu of South Africa, campaigned fervently for punitive international sanctions against his own country to force a change in its white supremacist policies.

"Apartheid cannot be reformed. It must be dismantled. You don't reform a Frankenstein, you destroy it."

Archbishop Desmond Tutu, to the United Nations, October 28, 1985

A funeral procession (opposite) winds through a township—euphemistically called a "homeland" by whites—bearing victims of a clash with police that left 15 black protesters dead.

Undermining Apartheid

The goal is that eventually there will be no black South Africans." So declared Minister of Black Affairs Cornelius Mulder after the imposition in 1948 of a system of racial separation and discrimination known by the Afrikaans word *apartheid*. Taken literally, Mulder's statement meant genocide, which the world would not allow. Yet what the world did tolerate for more than 40 years was a society in which the minority white population simply eradicated the black majority from the body politic. A slightly less repressive policy was imposed on the nation's Asian minorities—primarily from India—and on "colored," or mixed-race, residents.

Apartheid decreed that black South Africans—75 percent of the country's people—would live on 13 percent of the land, in 10 hardscrabble townships that they could leave only with passbooks to work at mostly menial jobs for appalling wages. They had no vote, no voice in their affairs; their education was minimal, their medical facilities worse. Slavery was not so very different.

There had been cries of outrage from the start, but whips, truncheons, and guns were powerful persuaders. In 1960, when blacks staged a passbook protest, police killed or wounded 249, and the government outlawed all activist groups. Over the next two decades, black leaders increasingly called for armed struggle. But others, notably Desmond Tutu *(left)*, an Anglican archbishop and 1984 Nobel Peace Prize winner, continued to preach nonviolence and a shift to a power-sharing racial union.

Yet by the mid-1980s the confrontations had become so frequent and so bloody that the government imposed a fiercely repressive emergency rule. South Africa's five million whites and 24 million blacks seemed headed for cataclysm—until in 1989 a pragmatic new president, F. W. de Klerk, stepped back from the brink by initiating serious talks with blacks.

A light had appeared in the darkness. Six months after de Klerk took office, Nelson Mandela, a leader of the outlawed African National Congress, the foremost black resistance group, would be released from 27½ years of imprisonment. Mandela's release foreshadowed sweeping changes: Apartheid laws would begin to fall in 1991, and three years later, in the country's first multiracial election, Nelson Mandela himself would become president of South Africa.

Ecological Disaster

Murphy's Law was working overtime. The supertanker's skipper was an alcoholic who was drinking in his cabin; the third mate, unqualified for command, was at the helm and was confused about the ship's position; the Coast Guard, saddled with outdated radar, lost the ship but issued no alarms; the owners had failed to install an emergency plan; and the Alaskan government had accepted the owners' glib assurances of safe operations at face value.

Thus was the situation on the night of March 24, 1989, when the *Exxon Valdez* ran aground in Alaska's Prince William Sound, ripping open its hull and spilling 11 million gallons of crude oil, precipitating the worst environmental accident in U.S. history. Over the next month the gunk spread across 1,800 square miles, devastating commercial fishing and destroying wildlife: In the final tally, 580,000 birds *(inset)* and 5,500 sea otters perished. Exxon eventually mounted a $2 billion cleanup and was also ordered to pay $5 billion in damages to fishermen. "Sure, Exxon may pay in the end," said one cannery owner. "But we sweated blood to build this place. Everyone in the Sound feels violated."

Spoiling the scenic beauty of snowcapped mountains marching down to the sea, a canvas containment barrier stretches across polluted waters. The black object in the foreground is a pump.

The Face of Homelessness

Whether homeless Americans numbered 350,000 or 3.5 million, it was a sad commentary on society that hordes of them roamed the streets with all their possessions, like the New York City woman at right. Many were alcoholics or addicts; many others were once-solid citizens victimized by circumstance.

A recession in 1982 had hiked unemployment. Meanwhile, President Reagan was downsizing government—and the ax fell heavily on programs for food, housing, and medical care. Aggravating the problem, since 1955 nearly 450,000 mental patients had been released from public institutions in the name of civil liberties. Many had adjusted, but an appalling 35 percent had not; they were the army of obviously disturbed people wandering helplessly, hopelessly until they died. As the decade came to a close, only meager relief efforts were available for this problem without a visible solution.

William Britton and his family camp in an open space outside Gallup, New Mexico, at the culmination of a yearlong job hunt that started in Michigan. The family's slender hopes would ride on Britton's new job in a mine—at a pay rate of $3.50 an hour.

The Fall of the Berlin Wall

At the stroke of midnight on November 9, 1989, the crowds of East Berliners let out a roar of triumph and started pouring through and up and over the grim barrier. Equally jubilant West Berliners greeted them with handshakes, hugs, and kisses; the whoops and popping of champagne corks lasted through the night. By dawn, the Berlin Wall, that detestable symbol of Communist tyranny and a divided Germany, had passed into history.

The speed of the collapse stunned the world. Only nine months before, East Germany's party chieftain, Erich Honecker, had been talking about the 28-year-old wall remaining in place for another century. But with reform sweeping the U.S.S.R., citizens of the countries long oppressed by the Soviets demanded freedom—now.

Tides of change had already engulfed Hungary and Poland, and the rest of the Eastern Bloc showed signs of rapidly giving way. East Germany's rulers figured their only hope was to open the jailhouse doors a crack by reining in their murderous border guards. In a twinkling, the trickle of East Germans crossing over became a flood.

Within 48 hours nearly two million people had visited the West, and many did not return. Now a new cry rose in German throats, a cry for reunification. And while that might worry those with memories of the Germany of Adolf Hitler, it was simply a matter of time until it happened.

The concrete chips fly as an East German takes a sledge to the Berlin Wall. "I don't feel like I'm in prison anymore," cried one young man.

Music for the Video Age

★

ROCK'S NEW MASS MEDIUM

I want my MTV" was the slogan of the world's first rock video TV network and the salvation of the recording industry. By 1979 pop music had fragmented, and record sales were plummeting. Programming on radio, the medium that brought rock to the masses, had splintered into a variety of narrow formats, each tightly bound by its playlists. Musically, MTV started out in 1981 in the same mode, with a mainstream format that, among its other effects, virtually excluded black performers. Within two years, however, the 24-hour cable network, by now reaching 17.5 million homes nationwide, had diversified its content.

Ironically, considering its virtually white-only beginnings, MTV got an immense boost from the talent and creativity of an African American performer. Michael Jackson *(right)* brilliantly reinvented the music video—till then little more than a promotional tool for selling records—converting it into a dazzling visual performance medium.

Others who might have languished in musical niches—new-wave artists, heavy-metal holdovers, country music traditionalists, timeless balladeers, and innovative rappers—were also able to broaden their appeal after finding a place on MTV or one of the other video music networks it spawned. As Keith Richards of the Rolling Stones put it, rock and roll and TV had "gotten married and can't leave each other alone."

Michael Jackson's riveting 1983 video of his monster hit "Thriller" brought black music belatedly into play on MTV. In the words of producer Quincy Jones, Jackson "connected with every soul in the world."

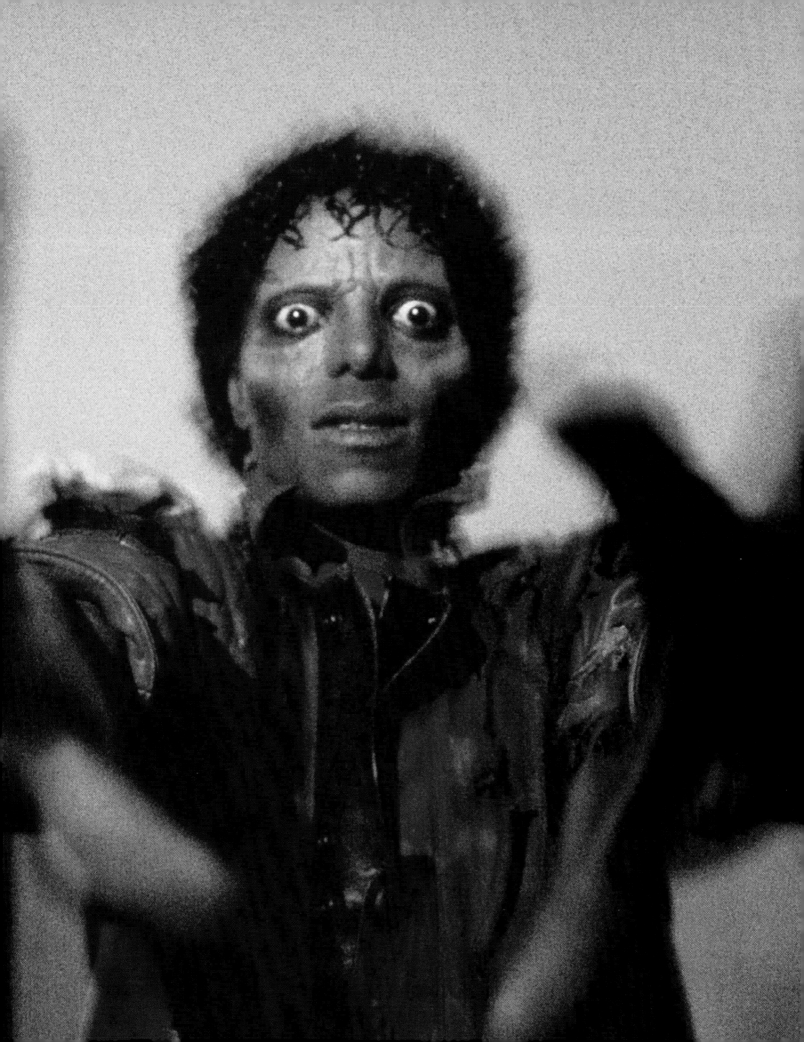

Michael and Madonna

They were the prom king and queen of the '80s—the couple who best represented past achievement, future promise, and the vitality of the here and now. No guy looked better on the dance floor than Michael Jackson, whose polished moves reflected his years as the nimble boy wonder of the Jackson 5. And for stage presence no girl in her class could rival Madonna, who shot from obscurity to superstardom by flaunting her sexuality—and making fun of it. Madonna, as actress Bette Midler quipped, "pulled herself up by her bra straps."

Jackson's reign as the King of Pop was solidified in late 1982 with the release of *Thriller*. Selling more than 40 million copies, it was the most successful recording in history. He was even more thrilling onstage and on video, prancing to the beat of hits like "Billie Jean." Jackson drew inspiration from dancer Fred Astaire, who returned the compliment. "My Lord," exclaimed Astaire, "he's a wonderful mover."

Televangelist Jerry Falwell sniffed that Jackson's sexually ambiguous look made him "a very bad role model" for children. But the soft-spoken singer was prim and presentable compared with Madonna, whose wildly popular album *Like a Virgin*, featuring her theme song, "Material Girl," rode the charts in 1985 amid a video blitz that inspired hordes of girls called wannabes to model themselves after her. Unfazed by charges that Madonna was antifeminist, the wannabes loved their Material Girl because she was sharp, sassy, and in control. "From when I was very young," Madonna confided, "I just knew that being a girl and being charming in a feminine sort of way would get me a lot of things, and I have milked it for everything I could."

Shy offstage, Michael Jackson lit up at showtime, delighting audiences with his stylish garb, trademark white glove, and moonwalk.

"If people don't get the humor in me or my act, then they don't want to get it."

Madonna, 1985

The bad girl of the '80s, Madonna made the most of her sexuality, teasing audiences with slinky outfits and sly gestures.

Rock Rides a New Wave

The rock scene of the '80s was an appealing blend of the old and the new. Fading stars cut fresh tracks and revived their careers, while brash newcomers recombined familiar musical elements to produce original statements. Among the decade's early hits was an album that marked the passing of an era, *Double Fantasy (page 122),* by Yoko Ono and the late John Lennon.

Meanwhile, a rising generation of rockers were reacting against the '70s punk scene—which survived in modified form among groups like Devo—by evolving a new-wave sound. The Police, a British group with the charismatic Sting as lead singer, disarmed listeners in 1980 by applying a catchy reggae beat to their breakthrough hit, "Don't Stand So Close to Me," a tale of erotic tension that set the stage for the group's 1983 blockbuster, "Every Breath You Take." Also topping the charts were Dire Straits and the Pretenders, groups made up of fine musicians who owed their success more to their distinctive sound and telling lyrics than to performance antics.

Few who rode the new wave to stardom, however, did so without offering something flashy to catch the eye. Deborah Harry, the former beautician and Playboy Club bunny whose bleached tresses distinguished the group Blondie, paved the way for Madonna by glamorizing rock. Cyndi

Sting

Boy George

Prince

Lauper sported orange hair as she unleashed her blissful classic of 1984, "Girls Just Want to Have Fun." Towering beehive hairdos gave the B-52s a retro look; their postpunk party music soared in 1980 with "Rock Lobster" and again in 1989 with the album *Cosmic Thing* and the hot single "Love Shack." Culture Club's driving force, Boy George, tried to go the girls one better with his cross-dressing getups, complimenting his fans on one occasion for recognizing "a good drag queen when you see one."

Although MTV carried Boy George, the station banned a video of "Who's That Girl" by the Eurythmics in which Annie Lennox removed a long-haired wig to reveal mannish-looking close-cropped tresses. Few rock stars of the '80s were more provocative than Prince, who blended an overtly sexual, new-wave persona with a rhythm-and-blues sense that earned him comparison with Stevie Wonder and Jimi Hendrix.

As the decade continued, success on the rock scene seemed to depend less on concocting something new than on refining time-honored formulas. ZZ Top, a self-described "little old blues band from Texas" that formed in 1970, kept the flame alive and finally hit it big in 1983 with their album *Eliminator*. George Michael emulated the soul singers of old and became the first white artist to top *Billboard*'s rhythm-and-blues chart with his 1987 album *Faith*. And veteran rocker Phil Collins scored repeatedly with danceable tunes like his 1983 remake of "You Can't Hurry Love" and sensitive love ballads like 1985's "One More Night." Other groups hit pay dirt by reviving heavy metal, with its grinding guitars and glaring exhibitionism. David Lee Roth, former Van Halen lead singer, bared his emotions—and his backside—in concert. Mining the same vein were Guns n' Roses, with their grungy look, and Mötley Crüe, which grabbed attention by claiming to worship Satan.

At the opposite end of the emotional spectrum was the uplifting Irish band U2— hailed for their 1987 album *The Joshua Tree*—whose lead singer, Bono, professed Christianity and sympathy for the downtrodden. John Cougar Mellencamp's lyrics brought attention to the hardships of life in small-town midwestern America with his 1982 album *American Fool*, which stayed at number one on the charts for nine weeks. And newcomer Bruce Hornsby, whose musical influences ranged from blues to bluegrass, explored race relations in his stirring 1986 debut, "The Way It Is."

The eclectic '80s offered equal opportunity to artists over 30. Tina Turner, who had children older than some of the decade's stars, made a comeback as a rock goddess with the release in 1984 of *Private Dancer*, in which she posed the provocative question "What's Love Got to Do With It?" Paul Simon, riding three decades of success, explored new ground in 1986 by joining with South African musicians on the Grammy-winning *Graceland*. And Bruce Springsteen, hailed as the "Boss" in the mid-'70s, triumphantly defended that title a decade later with *Born in the U.S.A.*, a rousing tribute to blue-collar America, where people rolled with the punches and came bouncing back—much like the Boss himself.

Mötley Crüe

David Lee Roth

Tina Turner

U2, *The Joshua Tree*

JOHN COUGAR *American Fool*

Bruce Springsteen

George Michael, *Faith*

BRUCE HORNSBY
AND THE RANGE

the way it is

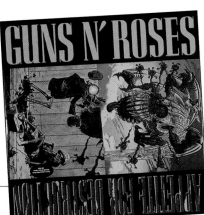

Refashioning the Love Ballad

I sing about the things that people tend to think about a lot," said Luther Vandross, who set hearts throbbing in the '80s with "It's Over Now" and other romantic ballads. "Everybody can identify with these situations." And almost everyone did, judging by record sales. In a phenomenon labeled by radio marketers the "quiet storm," Vandross and other soulful balladeers won huge followings across racial and generational lines by wrapping velvet vocals around passionate lyrics. Vandross caressed listeners with his sensual baritone. Anita Baker moved up and down the scales with smoky passion on her jazzy 1986 debut album, *Rapture*. And the irrepressible Whitney Houston *(right),* armed with a voice of operatic power, exploded onto both pop and soul charts with her 1985 single "You Give Good Love."

When it came to romancing the audience, few rock stars could rival two other balladeers. Spanish crooner Julio Iglesias *(inset, above)* enchanted older, mostly female fans by emulating the suave singing idols of the '40s and '50s. When asked how he managed to connect with his followers, he replied simply, "I seduce them."

The bard of the romantic singer-songwriters was Lionel Richie *(inset, left).* After breaking in with the Commodores, for whom he wrote such classics as "Three Times a Lady," Richie went solo in 1982 and racked up awards and acclaim for a string of hits that included two movie themes, "Endless Love" and "Say You, Say Me" (featured in the 1985 film *White Nights*). Richie caught the assertive mood of the day by crafting love songs that were not just "about a boy and a girl," as he put it, but that quietly encouraged listeners to "stand and be strong."

Whitney Houston made everyone feel like joining in when she belted out hits like "How Will I Know" and "I Wanna Dance With Somebody." As her producer put it, "She can get the kids on the dance floor, then turn around and reach your grandmother."

Sawing the fiddle and singing into his trademark old-time microphone, Ricky Skaggs performs in 1985 with the passion that made him the Country Music Association's Entertainer of the Year.

Bringing Country Back Home

While pop music in the '80s was branching out, Nashville, thanks to a new crop of young performers with old-time appeal, was getting over its recent fling with country rock and returning to its roots. Leading the way was Emmylou Harris. Harris must have seemed an unlikely savior to country fans pining for a return to musical traditions. Born in Alabama but raised in a Washington, D.C., suburb, she left college to play folk music in the '60s. Her crystalline soprano and solid guitar playing combined with her intelligence and delicate beauty to bring her success. But if her pedigree seemed upscale, her musical passions were down-home. She revered the harmonies of the Louvin Brothers and the Carter Family, working their classics into her repertoire by the late '70s.

Harris also emulated the likes of Kitty Wells, Loretta Lynn, and Dolly Parton, later hooking up with Parton and Linda Ronstadt (below) to record a million-selling album. In 1980 she was voted Female Vocalist of the Year by the Country Music Association, encouraging others to reinterpret older music. Among the best of these new traditionalists was Kentuckian Ricky Skaggs (left), who, after an apprenticeship with bluegrass legend Ralph Stanley, played backup with Harris for three years before making his own way in the early '80s. A former child sensation who had played mandolin with bluegrass originator Bill Monroe at the age of six, Skaggs drew listeners with his high-lonesome tenor and fancy picking.

Other hot new acts of the decade that exuded old-time charm were the mother-daughter duo the Judds (top right) and Randy Travis (right, center), whose gritty, gut-wrenching vocals, sung in a deep, honey-toned, nasal voice, won him comparisons with Merle Haggard.

Naomi Judd and daughter Wynonna (right) got their big break in 1983 after singing for a producer whose child Naomi had cared for.

In 1981 Randy Travis was working in Nashville—slinging hash. "I didn't know if I belonged there or not," he recalled, but within five years the young man with the weathered voice was the toast of the town.

Emmylou Harris (center) harmonized with Linda Ronstadt (left) and Dolly Parton on the album Trio in 1987. Ronstadt said that while she and Harris came to country as adults, Parton "crawled out of her cradle singing that music."

Trumpeter Wynton Marsalis honors jazz tradition by playing at the feet of Louis Armstrong's statue in a New Orleans park. Armstrong and other giants inspired the classically trained Marsalis, who said he learned the "jazz vocabulary by listening to records and watching other musicians."

Jazz Purists and Popularizers

Jazz, like country, staged a return to its roots in the '80s, led by a young virtuoso trumpeter, Wynton Marsalis. New Orleans, the birthplace of jazz, was Marsalis's home, and he never lost touch with it. As a teenager studying horn in the '70s, he imbibed pure acoustic jazz from recordings and from his father, pianist Ellis Marsalis, at a time when the synthesized sounds of funk and fusion were rocking the jazz world. "I don't like it when pop is sold as jazz," he remarked later after recording his first album. Instead, he set about reviving the music that New Orleans had made famous.

Marsalis mastered the classical repertoire before he turned to jazz, performing a trumpet concerto with the New Orleans Symphony Orchestra at the age of 14. Three years later, in 1979, he headed for New York and soon earned a full scholarship to the Juilliard School. Before he had completed his first term he was jamming with Art Blakey's Jazz Messengers, and he went on to perform with pianist Herbie Hancock. Of these experiences he said, "Playing with them was like walking on water."

Hancock produced Marsalis's well-received debut album in 1982. A year later, Marsalis scored an unprecedented double triumph when his second jazz album, *Think of One,* and his recording of classical trumpet concertos earned him Grammy awards in both the classical and jazz categories. At the ceremony, he thanked Louis Armstrong, Charlie Parker, and other jazz legends who, he said, "gave an art form to the American people."

Meanwhile, vocal gymnast Bobby McFerrin *(right)* went his own way, defying the distinctions that Wynton Marsalis tried to preserve by blending jazz with pop—to the delight of audiences. McFerrin, the son of the first African American man to sing a major part with the Metropolitan Opera, shared with Marsalis a grounding in classical music, but the similarity ended there. Rather than following in the footsteps of his father or of jazz greats, he made up his own sound that fused elements of scat, funk, calypso, bebop, and Bach, sung a cappella in a magical voice that spanned four octaves. McFerrin won the Best Male Jazz Vocalist Grammy for three years running and lifted America's spirits in 1988 with his infectious feel-good pop hit, "Don't Worry, Be Happy."

"I distinctly heard a voice inside my mind telling me to be a singer."

Bobby McFerrin

Jazz vocalist Bobby McFerrin, once a keyboard player, said that in 1977 he heeded a command from within to use the instrument God gave him.

The streetwise rap of Run-D.M.C. (above) paved the way for rap activists like Flavor Flav (below, left) and Chuck D (below, right) of Public Enemy, whose goal was to educate as well as entertain.

Rap Comes Knocking

Rap music swept nostalgia aside and laid down a tough new beat for the '80s. Consisting of strongly syncopated, sometimes controversial lyrics, spoken rather than sung against a raw rhythmic backdrop, rap evoked the urban black experience. "It's a whole new subculture that's been invented by the disenfranchised," remarked producer Quincy Jones, "and it's the freshest thing that's happened musically in 30 years."

Born in 1979 with the innocuous "Rapper's Delight," by the Sugar Hill Gang, rap, based on hard tales of street life in the inner city, matured in the early '80s. The masters of this tough talk were Run-D.M.C. *(left, top),* a trio from New York who scored rap's first gold record in 1984 and carried the sound to the top of the charts in 1986 with their blockbuster album, *Raising Hell.* Rivaling the group in popularity, and sometimes appearing with them, was L.L. Cool J *(right),* whose stage name was short for "Ladies Love Cool James." The poised 17-year-old brought his hit single "I Can't Live Without My Radio" to the big screen in 1985 in *Krush Groove,* the first rap movie.

Rap concerts were occasionally marred by violence, and the music grew even more controversial with the emergence of "gangsta" rappers, who filled their songs with obscenity and images of violence, rage, and the degradation of women. A backlash was inevitable. Taking the lead were the rap activists Public Enemy *(left, bottom),* who called for black unity and commitment in their top-selling protest album, *It Takes a Nation of Millions to Hold Us Back.* Female rappers joined in, starting with Queen Latifah, who talked back at the gangstas in her 1989 debut album, *All Hail the Queen.* By decade's end, even some of the toughest-talking rappers were joining stars like L.L. Cool J in discouraging violence.

Self-described mike "dominator" L.L. Cool J, onstage in 1987, displays the charisma that made him rap music's first sex symbol.

TV's Big Three Face Competition

★

THE BRAVE NEW WORLD OF CABLE

I n the early 1980s network TV's stranglehold on the viewing audience came under serious attack from new entertainment choices: movies on videocassette, independent stations, and—most threatening of all—cable. Gerald Levin of Time Inc.'s young cable entertainment network, Home Box Office (HBO), had in 1975 taken the bold step of sending out HBO's signal by satellite, making it more accessible to local cable systems. Then, in 1980, entrepreneur Ted Turner launched the Cable News Network (CNN). By 1985 almost half of America's households were receiving cable—double the rate of just five years earlier.

The networks needed something new to meet the challenge. NBC executives took the first risks. In addition to offering the usual network fare, they went after a narrower, upscale audience by exploring unconventional genres, controversial subjects, and offbeat characters.

They also, in 1984, breathed new life into the tired old sitcom format, with Bill Cosby as Dr. Cliff Huxtable—obstetrician, husband of attorney Clair, and father of five kids—on *The Cosby Show.* Cosby not only treated weekly viewers to his wry observations but broke new social ground. Never before had a TV series portrayed an African American family that was well off, accomplished, and completely normal. *The Cosby Show* was ranked third in popularity its premier season and was the number one show on TV for the next four years.

No traditional bubbleheaded sitcom dad, Dr. Cliff Huxtable—played with subtle humor by Bill Cosby— offers Rudy, the youngest of his five children, a moment of eye contact and paternal wisdom.

The Ewing clan—featuring self-satisfied J. R. (right)—strike a pose against the backdrop of their spacious spread on the soap Dallas.

Delicious Evil in Prime Time

"Once you give up integrity, the rest is a piece of cake."

J. R. Ewing, chief villain of *Dallas*

The Reagan-era mentality created a perfect atmosphere for glitzy prime-time soaps. Popular shows such as *Dallas* and *Dynasty* offered viewers a weekly dose of intrigue and treachery against a backdrop of popping champagne corks, sparkling gems, and furs that cushioned the cruelest blows. These were sprawling sagas of fortune, failure, revenge, and lechery—always set on a very large chunk of ultra-pricey real estate. No script was without at least three of the seven deadly sins, no character was painted any shade of gray. Pillow talk was as likely to be about mergers, cartels, leveraged buyouts, and business betrayals as about romance or sex.

Though *Dallas,* the first of these dramas, premiered in 1978, it hit its stride in the early '80s, when the spirit of the times was beginning to be more in tune with the greed and deceit at South Fork, the Ewings' Texas home. The Ewing brood—foremost among them the grinning imp of the oil fields, J. R.—became stock characters for the genre. When the 1980 season ended with J. R. lying wounded on the floor *(inset)*, "Who shot J. R.?" became the summer's mantra.

Dynasty was *Dallas* against a Rocky Mountain backdrop, a chronicle of evil and greed in mile-high Denver. The series featured a character of scrumptious cunning— Alexis *(far right)*, ex-wife of zillionaire Blake Carrington— who was a foil to virtuous current wife, Krystle. All lacquered talons and shoulder pads, these women were natural antagonists, highlighting each season with the inevitable catfight set in a pool, mud puddle, or beauty parlor.

Dynasty

NBC's floppy-featured ALF, more formally known as Alien Life Form, was dubbed a "bigger star than Alpha Centauri" by the press.

Roseanne Barr plays it for laughs on the messy Conner kitchen set, with John Goodman as her better half, Dan. Goodman described her as an "anti-June Cleaver."

Shown as he first looked, when he appeared in brief spots on The Tracey Ullman Show in the late 1980s, the devilish Bart Simpson, already the bane of dad Homer's existence, stands poised to spin off into cartoon sitcom stardom.

MATT GROENING

Family and Crime Fill Prime Time

If prime-time soaps showed Americans a world of big bucks and high living, the decade's innovative comedy programs brought the audience back to earth, giving new meaning to the idea of the TV family. In 1987 the feisty new Fox network, seeking to muscle its way in among the big three with programming out on the raunchy end of the spectrum, introduced the snide and cynical Bundys—Al and Peg *(inset)* and their kids, Bud and Kelly—on *Married . . . With Children.* There was even an alien at the table: *ALF (left, top)* crashed into the TV home of the Tanners in 1986. There, for the next four years, he was the wisecracking manic who came to dinner.

Somewhat alien themselves were *The Simpsons*, featuring the 10-year-old ne'er-do-well Bart *(left, bottom)*, first brought to life on Fox's *Tracey Ullman Show.* This cartoon family got its own slot in 1989, winning an audience of adults as well as kids with a rich cast of characters and a stream of witty lines and throwaway sight gags.

Roseanne and Dan Conner *(left, center)* pumped some spunk into the family sitcom genre. Playing the mom, brash and tacky Roseanne Barr brought a sense of the genuine to each week's episode as her family navigated the choppy waters of working-class life. Roseanne on bills: "You pay the ones marked 'final notice' and you throw the rest away."

Laughs were on tap at *Cheers*, and the crowd at this Boston watering hole formed an odd family of its own *(right)* that kept America company for the better part of the decade. So many viewers bellied up to the bar "where

Cheers regulars (clockwise from bottom left)—beer-guzzling patron Norm, sensitive barmaid Diane, skirt-chasing bar owner Sam, country-boy bartender Woody, wise-guy patron Cliff, and, at center, pit-bull barmaid Carla—traded sharp-edged jibes.

everybody knows your name" that the show earned well over 100 Emmy nominations—more than any other prime-time series.

Young singles were the target of *thirty-something,* whose extended family of up-scale boomer-age friends and lovers *(below)* sighed and suffered—along, it seemed, with vast numbers of their counterparts in the viewing audience—through four seasons of affluent angst.

The '80s also brought a wave of crime shows. On *Magnum, P.I.,* Tom Selleck, as hunky Hawaii-based detective Thomas Magnum *(top right),* was a softer sell than the usual TV tough guy. Cops Sonny Crockett and Ricardo Tubbs cruised in designer threads, a Ferrari, and a hipper-than-thou attitude on *Miami Vice (top left),* while CBS's *Cagney & Lacey (center left)* featured the first serious attempt to portray female cops as principals.

Moonlighting (center right) aimed for a sexy sophistication, as detective duo Maddie Hayes (Cybill Shepherd) and David Addison (Bruce Willis) sniped their way through the weekly case, displaying sassy tempers and rapid-fire repartee that appealed to yuppies from coast to coast. The makers of *Hill Street Blues (opposite)* risked a more experimental approach, weaving layers of dialogue and background sound with story lines strung out over several episodes to create a sophisticated naturalism previously unseen on TV.

Miami Vice

Magnum, P.I.

Cagney & Lacey

Moonlighting

thirtysomething

Sgt. Phil Esterhaus, a cop with a heart—played by Michael Conrad until his death in 1983—ended each week's opening roll call on Hill Street Blues with the admonition "Let's be careful out there."

The Coarsening of TV Talk

T alk shows in the '80s changed to a format so extreme that one of the chief engineers of the transformation, flamboyant host Geraldo Rivera *(opposite, bottom)* declared, "I'm embarrassing myself." With confrontational guests, provocative hosts, and sometimes rabid audiences, some TV talk became virtually synonymous with raunchy confessions and outrageous behavior.

Pioneer of the open mike was Phil Donahue *(left, top)*, who started the genre in Dayton, Ohio, in 1967 and went national three years later. Donahue kept a fast pace and a straight face as his guests confessed to all manner of offbeat views and predilections. Oprah Winfrey *(left, center)* brought the perspectives of a black woman to her mostly female audiences, discussing her victimization by sexual abuse, her drug history, and her diet wars. The over-the-top end of the spectrum, however, was occupied by Rivera's *Geraldo* and *The Morton Downey, Jr. Show (opposite, top)*. Both hosts invited the raggediest fringes of society to mix it up—sometimes literally—on the air.

Going strictly for laughs was David Letterman *(inset)*, whose *Late Night* show interspersed guests' chatter with bits like the "Top 10 List" and "Stupid Pet Tricks." Most unlikely host of all was an elfin Jewish grandmother named Ruth Westheimer *(right)*, who ladled out graphic sexual advice like chicken soup on her cable show, *Dr. Ruth*. To one caller whose girlfriend had given him an inflatable woman she said, "Give the doll a name and have a good time."

Host Phil Donahue wades into his audience in search of a connection. Donahue's inclusive salutation—"Caller, are you with us?"— and cocked ear assured viewers he was listening.

Her first name, for her fans, was sufficient: "Oprah." A bundle of energy, she radiated a warmth and empathy that made female viewers of all ages feel they were truly "girlfriends."

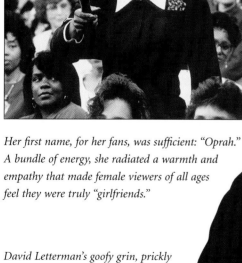

David Letterman's goofy grin, prickly wit, and nutty stunts—like donning a Velcro suit and jumping at a Velcro wall—won him a large slice of the young adult audience.

Morton Downey Jr.'s gaping maw frequently spewed insults. Too obnoxious even for fun, his nationally syndicated shoutfest lasted 14 months.

Geraldo Rivera brought a panel of white supremacists together with black activist Roy Innis in 1988—resulting in a broken nose for the host.

"Dr. Ruth" Westheimer's "tell me where it hurts" tone and grandmotherly warmth helped callers with thorny private issues. The four-foot-seven-inch thrice-married psychologist held forth on problems from impotence to infidelity.

Culture Becomes a Megabusiness

★

I dream for a living," Hollywood wunderkind Steven Spielberg said in the mid-'80s. "Once a month the sky falls on my head, I come to, and I see another movie I want to make." Among the producer-director's most lucrative dreams was the idea for the 1982 smash hit *E.T.: The Extra-Terrestrial*. At the movie's climax the lovable alien suspends the law of gravity, and his young rescuer bicycles him across the heavens *(left)*.

That striking image was emblematic of what was happening on many fronts in the world of art and entertainment: It was a decade of seeming levitation. Among other forms of uplift, the financial payoff for creativity rose to unimaginable heights. Spielberg's winsome tale of E.T., for example, grossed more than a billion dollars, making it the greatest money spinner in film history.

Book publishing followed a similar trajectory. In the 1970s, the only nonfiction book to sell more than a million copies was *The Living Bible*. The '80s saw that mark surpassed repeatedly—and never faster than by *Fatherhood (inset)*, Bill Cosby's take on the challenges of parenting, which sold 2.4 million copies in 1986 alone. On Broadway, too, bigness—in both costs and revenues—was being redefined. In 1980, a splashy musical required about $1 million to bring to the stage; a few years later, the figure was four or five times higher. But theater seats that went for $10 in the mid-'70s were selling for $25 to $45 by the next decade—and people lined up for hours to buy them.

Perhaps the most astonishing levitation of all, fueled by a robust economy, took place in the fine arts. A Picasso self-portrait that sold for $5.83 million in 1981 changed

---

Freed from gravity by the powers of the alien riding on his handlebars, the 10-year-old hero of Steven Spielberg's E.T.: The Extra-Terrestrial pedals across a moon-filled sky in a memorable getaway scene.

Altered personas, inspired costumes, and a dark art deco look were at the heart of Batman (above). The hero is shown here in the high-tech nerve center of his Batcave amid video images of his arch-enemy, the Joker.

In the movie Tootsie, *Dustin Hoffman played an unemployable actor named Michael Dorsey who reinvents himself as spunky actress Dorothy Michaels to win a soap-opera part, touching off a hilarious series of misunderstandings.*

hands again at decade's end for $47.95 million. In 1987, Vincent Van Gogh's *Irises* brought $53.9 million, the highest price ever paid for a single work of art. A number of present-day artists, especially in New York, also cashed in on the boom.

For all the money going into it, the art world was still a mystery to most Americans. Not so with Hollywood. People knew what they wanted, and in the '80s they wanted light comedies, romances, fantasies, and thrill-a-minute action-adventure stories. Heroes and villains were back, some of them drawn from the pages of comic books. Superman battled bad guys and dallied with Lois Lane in a hugely successful series of films. An even bigger hit was Batman, who ranged across a gloomy Gotham City in the summer of 1989. With Michael Keaton as the Caped Crusader and Jack Nicholson playing a gleefully demented Joker, the film burst out of the starting blocks, selling $167 million worth of tickets in just a little over three weeks. Meanwhile, Batmania was stoked by storefuls of merchandise—clothes, sunglasses, pens, backpacks, coffee cups, toy Batmobiles, even Bat earrings.

Movie protagonists came in every imaginable guise during the '80s. In *Tootsie* (1982), Dustin Hoffman became a part-time transvestite to win a role in a soap opera. *Tootsie* set a box-office record for comedies, but its $100 million take was topped two years later by *Ghostbusters,* a romp starring Bill Murray and Sigourney Weaver in which four goofy parapsychologists fight to rid Manhattan of an infestation of phantoms.

In *Top Gun* (1986), heartthrob Tom Cruise played a cocky fighter pilot, gaining altitude with the help of a stirring soundtrack and a torrid romance with Kelly McGillis. *Lethal Weapon* (1987) had Mel Gibson as a wacky but ferocious plainclothes cop who, in the climactic scene, refuted the villain's claim that there were "no heroes left." One film detective even had to share the screen with animated figures: In 1988's *Who Framed Roger Rabbit? (page 168),* a flesh-and-blood Bob Hoskins visited a cartoon world to solve a murder mystery.

When it came to tapping the public appetite for thrills and high-contrast struggles between good and evil, nobody did it better than Steven Spielberg and his good friend and fellow producer-director George Lucas. In 1980 they were 33 and 36 years old, respectively, and both were already

In The Empire Strikes Back, the Jedi knight Yoda, rich in battle lore and spiritual strength, philosophized about the qualities needed to combat the evil spreading through the galaxy.

enormously rich and successful, Lucas having broken into the big time with his space epic *Star Wars* three years earlier and Spielberg sporting two blockbusters on his résumé, *Jaws* and *Close Encounters of the Third Kind.*

Over and over again during the '80s the two created gigantic hits. As producer of *The Empire Strikes Back* (1980), Lucas revisited the galactic scene of his previous hit, summoning back such starwarriors as the black-armored Darth Vader and the gritty Princess Leia and introducing the homely but endearing Yoda *(overleaf).*

The *Star Wars* series would go on, with *The Return of the Jedi* in 1983. Meanwhile, Lucas as producer and Spielberg as director embarked on what would be a swashbuckling adventure trilogy that one critic called "the Saturday afternoon serial in excelsis": In 1981 came *Raiders of the Lost Ark (inset),* followed by *Indiana Jones and the Temple of Doom* (1984) and *Indiana Jones and the Last Crusade*

(1989). These featured an archaeologist hero, sublimely evil villains, exotic locations, lost cities and treasures, romantic interludes, and other echoes of old-time attractions.

In their work together and separately, the two young moguls reshaped Hollywood's creative landscape. Lucas became a technology pioneer, the inventor of new sound-editing, film-editing, and special-effects techniques. Spielberg was a superbly gifted storyteller, nostalgic for past films and unafraid of sentiment. Between them they made six of the 10 most profitable films of the decade. When it came to sailing high and far, their accomplishments might have impressed even E.T.

Bob Hoskins as detective Eddie Valiant tries to free himself from his frantic Toon pal in Who Framed Roger Rabbit?, a dazzling meld of live actors and cartoons. The film was produced by Steven Spielberg for the Disney company; special effects were by George Lucas's Industrial Light and Magic.

Fearless archaeologist Indiana Jones—played by Harrison Ford—gallops after a German tank in a scene from Raiders of the Lost Ark, an action-laced tale of a hunt for the container holding the Ten Commandments. The role, said Harrison, was "probably the most fun I've ever had on a film."

"To survive war, you have to become war."

Macho hero John Rambo

Maestros of Mayhem

From the earliest days Hollywood had its he-men, but the action-movie genre of the '80s produced some versions that seemed to bubble over with testosterone. For sheer undiluted aggressiveness, nothing could top the robotic visitor from the future in *The Ter-*

His torso filling center screen, Arnold Schwarzenegger plays a killer robot in The Terminator. *Among his few lines was a deadpan "I'll be back," delivered to a desk sergeant at a police station where his quarry is being questioned. Moments later, he returns in a car and smashes into the station house.*

minator (1984). Played by former Mr. Universe Arnold Schwarzenegger, the brawny, monosyllabic killing machine *(left)* obliterated anyone who got in its way.

Most of the decade's ultramacho types were on the side of law and order, but often they had a loner's approach to their work that antagonized uptight authority. As the tough detective "Dirty Harry" Callahan in *Sudden Impact* (1983), Clint Eastwood was almost eager to blow away bad guys, taunting one malefactor with a line that became a popular expression: "Go ahead, make my day." In *Die Hard* (1988),

Bruce Willis played a scruffy and irreverent cop who single-handedly thwarts a group of well-armed bad guys.

Sylvester Stallone proved indomitable in two roles that he played repeatedly. One was Rocky, a boxer of limited talent but bottomless courage; the other was John Rambo, ex-Green Beret and a grandmaster of automatic weapons, grenades, and other noisy instruments of destruction. *Newsweek,* having described the Rocky films as "bloodbaths," sighed that the second Rambo movie *(below)* "makes the 'Rockys' look like 'Winnie-the-Pooh.' "

Assault weapon blazing, Sylvester Stallone triumphs in Rambo: First Blood, Part II (1985). In the film, Vietnam vet John Rambo is dropped into the Southeast Asian jungle to rescue abandoned prisoners of war. He does it alone, averaging—according to one appalled critic—161 violent acts per hour.

Fatal Attraction

Sweet Dreams

Peggy Sue Got Married

Out of Africa

Romance—Sweet and Otherwise

Time-honored romantic themes came back big in the '80s, repackaged for a permissive age. Among the most visually beautiful of the romances was *Out of Africa* (1985), based on an autobiographical book by Danish author Isak Dinesen. The movie presented Meryl Streep and Robert Redford as aristocratic lovers seeking happiness in the spectacular setting of colonial Kenya; it won seven Academy Awards. Even more traditional was *An Officer and a Gentleman* (1982), a promilitary, promarriage movie in which the heroine wins her man, ascending from factory worker to officer's wife.

Bliss was frequently absent, however, in Hollywood's treatments of gender relationships during the '80s. *Sweet Dreams* (1985), a more or less biographical film, traced the sadly tangled love life of country singer Patsy Cline. In *Peggy Sue Got Married* (1986), a woman contemplating divorce travels back in time to find out if she would marry the same man again.

Fatal Attraction (1987), labeled by a *Washington Post* reviewer "the feel-bad movie of the decade," went way beyond typical man-woman discord. Glenn Close played a New York book editor who becomes a homicidal stalker after being rejected by a married man (Michael Douglas) with whom she has a weekend affair. Coproducer Sherry Lansing said she knew she had a hit after a Manhattan psychoanalyst reported that a majority of his patients wanted to discuss the film in their therapy sessions. Average moviegoers found it unnerving too. Said one, "I saw a lot of couples looking at each other sideways as they walked out."

Richard Gere sweeps Debra Winger off her feet for the happy ending of An Officer and a Gentleman (right), portending a good old-fashioned marriage. But the film was updated with graphic premarital sex: When the actors are together, a critic wrote, "the screen exudes a palpable sexuality, a bona fide romantic ache."

A Rash of Slashers

Well aware that a vast teenage movie audience reveled in supernatural frights and blood-splattered shocks, grade B filmmakers inundated the 1980s with horror films designed just for youth. To the dismay of parents, feminists, and many reviewers, these highly profitable films only faintly resembled classics like *Frankenstein*, *Dracula*, or Alfred Hitchcock's 1960 thriller, *Psycho*. Instead, they followed a simple formula: Demented or supernatural serial murderer stalks teenage girls, young women, or children, then mutilates and kills them.

According to '80s horror-flick convention, anyone from a disturbed adolescent to a ghost could be a slasher; among the more unlikely ones were Santa Claus (*Silent Night, Deadly Night*, 1984) and a doll (*Child's Play*, 1988). Best of all, the formula could be revisited in sequel after moneymaking sequel. *Halloween*, which launched the genre in 1978, had four. *Friday the 13th* had seven.

Although there were attempts at raising production values—notably in *The Shining* (1980), with Jack Nicholson (*right*)—teen-oriented terror films could always get by on cheap thrills. Few movies offered more than *A Nightmare on Elm Street* (1984), in which disfigured Freddy Krueger (*below*), following his death in a fire, visits the dreams of teenagers. Anyone whose mind he enters is doomed to a ghastly death. In one scene, a bed swallows the victim, then spouts blood. The film became an instant camp classic.

Horribly scarred by burns and equipped with razor-tipped fingers, Freddy Krueger, played by Robert Englund, menaces a hapless teenage girl in A Nightmare on Elm Street (above). In The Shining a crazed Jack Nicholson (right) infuses the Tonight Show's famous line, "Here's Johnny," with a macabre humor. He portrays a writer driven mad by creative setbacks who slays several occupants of a rundown hotel with an ax.

Something for Everyone

Movie hits in the '80s updated every film genre—romantic comedy (Moonstruck), war (Platoon), farce (Airplane!), science fiction (Robocop), and more. Some movies, such as Raging Bull, delved into elemental emotions, but highbrow subjects worked well, too: Amadeus, for example, was based on a stage play about Mozart; it won the 1984 Oscar for best picture.

Heady Times on the Frontiers of Art

Energy and money were the story of the visual arts in the '80s. The New York studio and gallery scene saw artistic experimentation run rampant, and Wall Street's joyride flooded the city with cash in search of art. One of the decade's biggest names was Julian Schnabel, whose first show featured huge paintings with broken crockery embedded in the canvas *(below)*. "I wanted to make something that was exploding as much as I wanted to make something that was cohesive," he said. His price per painting certainly exploded—from $6,000 to $600,000 in five years.

Radiant Baby,
by Keith Haring

Many artists worked almost as hard at self-promotion as they did at being creative, and it brought some of them yearly sales of over $1 million. Incorporating pop culture into art was an enthusiasm for many, but Keith Haring reversed the flow. His cartoon-like images *(inset)* were not only for sale in galleries but also appeared on wrist watches, tote bags, and radios.

Boldly inventive architects like Michael Graves and Robert Venturi also made their mark, finding a market for "postmodernism"—a playful, ornamented approach that surpassed modernist austerity.

Michael Graves's Portland Building (1982) combined such classical references as triple tiers and rectangular shapes with vibrant color. The Oregon structure became an icon of postmodernism.

Keith Haring's Cup Man (left) exemplifies his graffiti-like style. Said Haring, "You can't just stay in your studio and paint."

Julian Schnabel's The Mud in Mudanza (1982) combined painting with shards of pottery. Hilton Kramer of the New York Times characterized Schnabel's work as "neo-expressionism." Another critic praised it as "a sculptural representation of an archeological site," whose themes were the flow of history and the rise and fall of cultures.

Hardcover Bestsellers

Nonfiction

1980 *Crisis Investing,* Douglas R. Casey—438,000

1981 *The Beverly Hills Diet,* Judy Mazel—756,000

1982 *Jane Fonda's Workout Book*—693,000

1983 *In Search of Excellence: Lessons from America's Best-Run Companies,* Thomas J. Peters and Robert H. Waterman—1,160,000

1984 *Iacocca: An Autobiography*—1,055,000

1985 *Iacocca: An Autobiography*—1,510,000

1986 *Fatherhood,* Bill Cosby—2,400,000

1987 *Time Flies,* Bill Cosby—1,461,000

1988 *The 8-Week Cholesterol Cure,* Robert E. Kowalski—961,000

1989 *All I Really Need to Know I Learned in Kindergarten: Uncommon Thoughts on Common Things,* Robert Fulghum—902,000

Fiction

1980 *The Covenant,* James Michener—553,000

1981 *Noble House,* James Clavell—489,000

1982 *E.T.: The Extra-Terrestrial Storybook,* William Kotzwinkle—666,000

1983 *Return of the Jedi Storybook,* Joan D. Vinge—882,000

1984 *The Talisman,* Stephen King and Peter Straub—880,000

1985 *The Mammoth Hunters,* Jean Auel—1,471,000

1986 *It,* Stephen King—1,206,000

1987 *The Tommyknockers,* Stephen King—1,405,000

1988 *The Cardinal of the Kremlin,* Tom Clancy—1,277,000

1989 *Clear and Present Danger,* Tom Clancy—1,625,000

Big books of the decade ranged from Pat Conroy's lush Prince of Tides (1986)—about a dysfunctional southern family—to Elvis and Me (1985), Priscilla Presley's memoir.

Bonanzas in the Book Market

As with Hollywood and the art market, a blockbuster mentality took hold of the book-publishing industry in the '80s. Spurred by aggressive promotion campaigns, mass market distribution, and widespread discounting, the top titles scaled increasingly dizzying sales heights as the decade progressed. (Strangely, the rise in boffo bestsellers was not enough to boost the industry as a whole; overall sales were flat.)

In 1980 the top fiction title was James Michener's *The Covenant;* its hardcover sales of better than half a million copies was considered huge. By 1989 Tom Clancy's *Clear and Present Danger* sold three times as many. The content of hot-selling fiction ranged across the escapist spectrum. Book buyers gobbled up the sex-and-shopping tales of Danielle Steele and Judith Krantz, the sweeping historical panoramas of James Michener and James Clavell, and the horror stories of Stephen King *(box, right).* Their products tended to be big in more ways than one: The hardcover version of Stephen King's *It*—the fiction pacesetter for 1986—was 1,138 pages long and weighed in at a wrist-straining three pounds, seven and a half ounces.

Some of the decade's bestsellers had can't-miss inevitability. For example, the 1982 fiction leader was a spinoff of the movie smash *E.T.: The Extra-Terrestrial.* The following year's top seller rode the coattails of *The Return of the Jedi,* latest in the *Star Wars* movies. But a few megahits seemed to come out of nowhere. One was *Presumed Innocent* (1987), a gripping tale of murder and its aftermath written by a little-known lawyer-turned-author named Scott Turow. Another surprise was *The Hunt for Red October* (1984), authored by Tom Clancy, an insurance agent and war-games buff. His book, which quickly became a monster bestseller, was released not by one of the powerhouse Manhattan publishers but by a quiet, scholarly organization called the Naval Institute Press and was the institute's first foray into fiction. To the utter delight of the industry, Clancy proved to be a writing machine, turning out immense hits at a steady clip. Most were instantly snapped up by Hollywood for translation to the big screen.

Nonfiction bestsellers reflected the decade's obsession with business success, money, and self-image. Nonfiction lists in the '70s had generally been heavy on history and biography. In the '80s the emphasis switched to getting ahead, making money, losing weight, and shaping up.

Master of the Macabre

The most successful author of the '80s was Stephen King, an unpretentious Mainer who gave new twists to the traditional Gothic horror genre. He portrayed everyday American small-town life—complete with malls, brand names, and proms. But this familiar reality was beset by shocks and terrors: haunted cars, fiends living in drains, monsters that overtook people's minds, buckets of blood, and an especially eerie graveyard (inset).

King, a workaholic, never seemed to run out of ideas. He wrote all day, every day except Christmas, Independence Day, and his birthday. So prodigious was his output—four behemoth novels in one 18-month stretch—that his publisher worried about overexposure. The solution was issuing a number of books under an alias, Richard Bachman.

By 1985 no fewer than 50 million copies of his books were in print, and he had earned more than $20 million. His fortune and fame would continue to grow, but success didn't diminish his work habits or erode his clear-eyed modesty. His books, he once said, were the "literary equivalent of a Big Mac and a large fries from McDonald's."

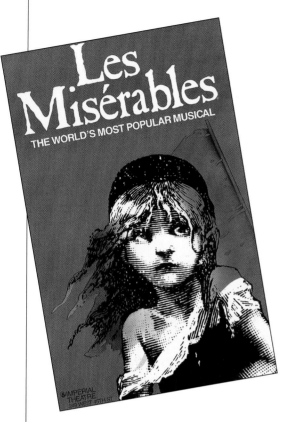

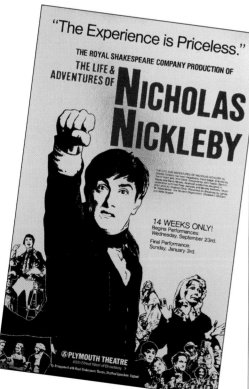

Lucrative Days on Broadway

Riding an economic resurgence and benefiting from infusions of British talent, Broadway boomed during the '80s. Audiences flocked to theatrical extravaganzas, beginning in 1981 with the Royal Shakespeare Company's *The Life and Adventures of Nicholas Nickleby (left, bottom)*, a staging of the Charles Dickens novel that required 39 actors playing 250 roles over an incredible eight and a half hours. Tickets cost $100. People lined up for them.

Most of the blockbusters were musicals, including a number of American offerings, such as *42nd Street* (1980), *Dreamgirls* (1981), and a revival of Cole Porter's *Anything Goes* (1987). But the leaders of the field were British, with composer Andrew Lloyd Webber *(pages 184-185)* heading the

---

"My work is about how the past must inform your future."

Playwright August Wilson

---

creative pack and producer Cameron Mackintosh showing the way in marketing. Nothing like Mackintosh's promotional campaigns had ever been seen in the American theater before. His presentation of *Les Misérables*—a musical version of the 19th-century Victor Hugo novel—was preceded by 10 months of full-page newspaper ads featuring a Parisian waif *(left, top)*; her image also adorned items ranging from coffee mugs to T-shirts. The reward was more than $11 million in advance ticket sales—a record.

Along with big musicals, Broadway produced a crop of thoughtful dramas, including Sam Shephard's *Fool for Love*, Neil Simon's *Brighton Beach* trilogy, and David Mamet's *Glengarry Glen Ross* and *Speed-the-Plow*. And the '80s saw the debut of August Wilson—"the theater's most astonishing discovery this decade," said the *New York Times*. His cycle of plays about the African American experience won every award and drew record audiences.

Vincent Gardenia (left) and Joe Mantegna star as corrupt real estate salesmen in David Mamet's brutal tragicomedy, Glengarry Glen Ross.

Bynum Walker (Ed Hall) urges Herald Loomis (Delroy Lindo) to transcend the tragic past in August Wilson's 1988 hit, Joe Turner's Come and Gone.

"She is deeply concerned with the ways of the mice—Their behavior's not good and their manners not nice."

From *Cats* (based on poems by T. S. Eliot)

Michael Crawford played the disfigured hero of Phantom of the Opera. His acting gave emotional heat to a show that was judged by the New York Times to be "as much a victory of dynamic stage-craft over musical kitsch as a triumph of merchandising über alles."

Andrew Lloyd Webber: Midas of Musicals

At the start of the '80s composer Andrew Lloyd Webber already had a few hit musicals under his belt, most notably *Jesus Christ Superstar* and *Evita.* By the end of the decade he was a veritable musical empire.

His dominance of Broadway, however, was not universally welcomed. "He writes only one melody per show and then builds a set around it," was a typical comment on Lloyd Webber's music, lyrics, and plots, which many critics considered thin. He was also known for almost legendary bad manners and temper tantrums.

His first truly huge hit was *Cats* (1982), built around *Old Possum's Book of Practical Cats,* a volume of light verse written by the poet T. S. Eliot in 1939. The show had little plot and its music was uneven, but the staging was astounding. The theater became a giant-scale junkyard, overarched by a fiberoptic starry sky from which a stairway to paradise magically descended. Audiences loved it. By 1989 *Cats* had set the record as the most profitable venture in the history of theater.

Meanwhile, the indefatigable composer had created more spectacles, among them a musical that was performed on roller skates, *Starlight Express* (1984). In 1988 came his seventh musical, based on a 1910 thriller, *The Phantom of the Opera.* Its sets included an underground lake, a subterranean vault illuminated by hundreds of candles, and a chandelier that swung over the audience and appeared to crash onto the stage. By opening night the show was sold out 10 months in advance.

The furry cast of Cats groups itself around Grizabella, a once-glamorous feline who has fallen on hard times. The musical, said the New York Times, "transports the audience into a complete fantasy world that could only exist in the theater and yet, these days, only rarely does."

ACKNOWLEDGMENTS

The editors wish to thank the following individuals and institutions for their valuable assistance in the preparation of this volume:
Margaret Adamic, Disney Publishing Group, Burbank, Calif.; Richard Allen, Lynden, Wash.; Judy and Ed Ashley, Jed Collectibles, Pemberton, N.J.; Henri Bailey, Herndon, Va.; Robert Blakeman, Los Angeles, Calif.; J. Grant Brittain, *TransWorld SKATEboarding,* Oceanside, Calif.; Wayne E. Carlson, Ohio State University, Columbus; Aimee S. Cass, NAMCO Holding Corp., San Jose, Calif.; Tom Conroy, Movie Still Archives, Harrison, Nebr.; Jeff Elmendorf, Funk & Junk, Alexandria, Va.; Michael Ferrell, Coalition for the Homeless, Washington, D.C.; Mike Gentry, NASA Media Services, Houston, Tex.; Kathy Hamor, L. L. Bean, Inc., Freeport, Maine; Tom Harlan, Nintendo Corp., Redmond, Wash.; Mary Ison and staff, Library of Congress, Washington, D.C.; Jim Marshall, San Francisco, Calif.; Ruth Porter, L. L. Bean, Inc., Freeport, Maine; Jim Powers, Ronald Reagan Library and Museum, Simi Valley, Calif.; Barbara Ann Rice, Cabin John, Md.; Sue Runfola, Apple Computers, Cupertino, Calif.; Lou Soucie, The Sharper Image, San Francisco, Calif.; Tom Way, IBM Corp., Essex Junction, Vt.

PICTURE CREDITS

The sources for the illustrations in this book appear below. Credits from left to right are separated by semicolons, from top to bottom by dashes.
Cover and dust jacket: Eddie Adams/Sygma, New York; Rick Friedman/Black Star, New York; Frank Fournier/Contact Press Images, New York; Michael Baytoff/Black Star, New York; John Zimmerman/*Sports Illustrated;* Douglas Kirkland/Sygma, New York; Mary Ellen Mark, New York—Michael Evans/Sygma, New York.
3: Reproduced from AMERICA A-Z, copyright © 1997 The Reader's Digest Association, Inc. Used by permission of The Reader's Digest Association, Inc., photo by Noel Allum. 6, 7: © 1983 Time Inc. Reprinted by permission; James Mason/Black Star, New York. 8, 9: Bruce McBroom. 10, 11: Steven E. Stutton/Duomo, New York. 12, 13: © Sal Lopes, Boston, Mass. 14, 15: Patrick Lichfield/Camera Press, London. 16, 17: Corbis/UPI/Bettmann. 18, 19: Bruce Weber, New York. 20, 21: NASA. 22: Manoocher/Sipa Press, New York. 23: SMP/Globe Photos, Inc., New York—Barry Staver/PEOPLE Weekly. PEOPLE Weekly is a registered trademark of Time Inc., used with permission. Ralph Morse/*Time* Magazine—ANSA, Rome. 24: Bill Fitz-Patrick, The White House. 25: FDA History Office, Rockville, Md.—John Madere; Ben Weaver; Bower/Sipa Press, New York—Fabian/Sygma, New York. 26: Courtesy Anne Whittle. 27: Love/Black Star; Harry Benson, New York, *Life* Magazine, © Time Inc.; Al Freni/*Life* Magazine—Gamma/Liaison Agency, New York. 28: Van de Walla/Liaison Agency, New York. 29: Igor Kostin/Imago/Sygma, New York; Dale Wittner, Seattle, Wash.; Greg Gibson/Corbis/UPI/Bettmann Newsphotos—courtesy *National Enquirer.* 30: Terry Ashe/Gamma/Liaison Agency, New York—Donna Bagby-*Dallas Times Herald*/Sipa Press, New York. 31: California Raisin Marketing Board; Rob Nelson; Burt Glinn/Magnum, New York—Bryn Colton. 32: © 1989 Time Inc. Reprinted by permission. 33: Stuart Franklin/Magnum, New York; Cynthia Johnson—Gary Bogdan/*Orlando Sentinel.* 34, 35: Charles Bennet-AP/Wide World Photos. 37: Tim Graham/Sygma, New York. 39: Tom Sobolik/Black Star, New York. 41: David Burnett/Contact Press Images, New York. 43: Howard Bingham/*Time* Magazine (4). 45: Mark Meyer. 46, 47: Brian Aris/Outline Press, New York. 49: © Harry Benson, New York. 50, 51: Courtesy Ronald Reagan Library, Simi Valley, Calif.; Michael Evans/Sygma, New York. 52: Courtesy Ronald Reagan Library, Simi Valley, Calif.; Corbis/Bettmann—Hershenson-Allen Archive, West Plains, Mo.—Movie Still Archives, Harrison, Nebr. 53: Photofest, New York. 54: AP/Wide World Photos. 55: Corbis/UPI/Bettmann—© 1981 Sebastiao Salgado/Contact Press Images, New York. 56: Courtesy Ronald Reagan Library, Simi Valley, Calif. 57: *Fortune* Magazine © Time Inc. 58: Peter Jordan/*Time* Magazine. 59: Diana Walker, *Time* Magazine © Time Inc.; © 1987 Time Inc. Reproduced by permission. 60, 61: *The New York Times.* Reproduced with permission; © Neil Leifer, New York. 62, 63: Patrick Demarchelier. 63: Courtesy Funk & Junk at http://www.funkandjunk.com. 64: Private collection; Rolex Oyster Perpetual Day-Date in 18 karat gold (R182388), courtesy Rolex Watch U.S.A., Inc.—Cuisinart Corporation—courtesy Myrna E. Traylor. 65: © 1986 L. L. Bean, Freeport, Maine—courtesy The Sharper Image, San Francisco, Calif.; Al Freni/*Life* Magazine; © 1982 Bob Glasheen/Photophile, San Diego, Calif.—John Dominis, *Life* Magazine © Time Inc.—BMW of North America, Woodcliff Lake, N.J. 66: Lester Sloan/Liaison Agency, New York; West Stock, Seattle, Wash.—© Nicholas DeVore III-Photographers/Aspen, Inc.; © Tony Perrottet/Omni-Photo Communications, New York—© 1988 Bart Bartholomew/Black Star, New York. 67: ZEFA-U.K./H. Armstrong Roberts, Philadelphia, Pa. 68: James Wojcik (2)—Al Freni/*Life* Magazine; James Wojcik (2)—reproduced from AMERICA A-Z, copyright © 1997 The Reader's Digest Association, Inc. Used by permission of The Reader's Digest Association, Inc., photo by Noel Allum. 69: Photos of MASTERS OF THE UNIVERSE® character toys provided courtesy of Mattel, Inc. (2); J. Grant Brittain/TransWorld SKATEboarding Magazine, Oceanside, Calif.; courtesy Funk & Junk at http://www.funkandjunk.com (3)—Christopher Morris/Black Star, New York—Al Freni/*Life* Magazine; courtesy Eloise Kelley; James Keyser/Sygma, New York. 70, 71: Mark Sennet; photograph by Harry Benson, inset © Steve Schapiro/Black Star, PEOPLE Weekly. PEOPLE Weekly is a registered trademark of Time Inc., used with permission—courtesy Video Vault, Alexandria, Va. 72: Neal Preston—Photofest, New York; The Kobal Collection, New York. 73: John Shannon; James A. Palmer Enterprises, by CMG Worldwide, Inc.—no credit. 74: © Jeff Greenberg/The Picture Cube, Boston, Mass.—© Beckman/Retna Ltd., New York. 75: Globe Photos, Inc., New York. 76, 77: Sculpture by George Segal, computer by Richardson/Smith Design, photograph by Roberto Brosan; IBM Corporation, photograph by Tom Way. 78: William Thompson, Microsoft, Seattle, Wash.—Forrest M. Mims III, Sequin, Tex. 79: Apple Computer, Inc., Cupertino, Calif.; Margaret Wozniak, courtesy Apple Computer, Cupertino, Calif.—© Chuck O'Rear/Woodfin Camp & Associates, New York. 80: Mark Perlstein; no credit—Gabe Palmer/Palmer/Kane, Inc.,The Stock Market, New York; no credit. 81: Casio Inc., Dover, N.J.; no credit (3)—IBM Corporation, Thornwood, N.Y. 82: Hitachi Ltd., Tokyo, Japan; Tom Wolff, Glen Echo, Md.—Daimler-Chrysler, Stuttgart. 83: Skidmore, Owings & Merrill LLP—R.Feldmann/Dan McCoy/Rainbow, Housatonic, Mass. (3); Nelson L. Max/LLNL & Arthur Olson/LBNL, U.S. Department of Energy, Lawrence Livermore National Laboratory, Livermore, Calif. 84: Mario Ruiz/Phototake, New York, insets PAC-MAN TM © 1980 NAMCO Ltd., all rights reserved. Courtesy of NAMCO Holding Corp. 85: © 1998 Nintendo image courtesy of Nintendo of America Inc. 86: Hsuen Ho, Advanced Computing Center for the Arts and Design, Ohio State University, Columbus, Ohio—© Disney Enterprises, Inc. Transparency courtesy Movie Still Archives, Harrison, Nebr. 87: No credit. 88, 89: © 1985 Time Inc. Reprinted by permission; © 1988 Joseph Rodriguez/Black Star, New York. 90: No credit; private collection. 91: Louis Psihoyos/Matrix, New York—© Gerardo Somoza/Outline Press, New York. 92: © 1988 Time Inc. Reprinted by permission—© Warner Bros. Inc., courtesy Photofest, New York. 93: Jonathan Levine—Photofest, New York. 94: © Terry Ashe/Sygma, New York. 95: Gamma/Liaison Agency, New York. 96, 97: AFP photo by Maria Bastone; © 1987 Tom Sobolik/Black Star, New York. 98, 99: Heinz Kluetmeier/*Sports Illustrated; The Sporting News,* St. Louis, Mo. 101: © Neil Leifer, New York. Tony Duffy/Allsport, New York. 102: Walter Iooss/*Sports Illustrated.* 103: Mike Powell/Allsport, New York. 104: John Biever/*Sports Illustrated*—courtesy Paul and Sylvia Gayer. 105: Al Messerschmidt, Tarpon Springs, Fla. 106: Steve Lipofsky, Nahant, Mass. 107: Richard Mackson, Los Angeles, Calif. 108, 109: Paul Bereswill/*Sports Illustrated.* 110, 111: Heinz

Kluetmeier/*Sports Illustrated*, except bottom left, Ronald C. Modra/ *Sports Illustrated*. **112:** Focus on Sports/*Sports Illustrated*—Chuck Solomon/*Sports Illustrated*. **113:** Ronald C. Modra/*Sports Illustrated*. **114:** Tony Duffy/Allsport, New York; Manny Millan/*Sports Illustrated*. **115:** Gouverneur/Gamma/Liaison Agency, New York—Richard Mackson/ *Sports Illustrated*. **116, 117:** © Neil Leifer, New York; Ken Regan/Camera 5, *Sports Illustrated* © Time Inc.. **118, 119:** Daniel Simon/Liaison Agency, New York; Jake Rajs/*Life* Magazine. **120:** NASA. **121:** Michele McDonald. **122:** Evan Agostini/Liaison Agency, New York. **123:** D. Goldberg/Sygma, New York. **124:** Rob Levine, Time, Inc. **125:** Chuck Fishman/*Time* Magazine (9). **126, 127:** Alon Reininger, Contact Press Images, New York; Lee Snider/Photo Images, New York. **128, 129:** Chuck Nacke; © Mark Downey/Viesti Collection, Durango, Colo. **130, 131:** Selwyn Tait/*Time* Magazine. **132, 133:** Randy Brandon/Sipa Press, New York; B. Nation/Sygma, New York. **134:** Copyright Joel Sternfeld. Courtesy PaceWildensteinMacGill, New York. **135:** © Alon Reininger/ Contact Press Images, New York. **136, 137:** Alexandra Avakian/Woodfin Camp & Associates, New York. **138, 139:** Movie Still Archives, Harrison, Nebr.; Douglas Kirkland/Sygma, New York. **140:** Ben Weaver (2); Sam Emerson (2)—Ben Weaver (2). **141:** © Topham/The Image Works, Woodstock, N.Y. **142:** Michael Putland/Retna Ltd., New York; Michael Ochs Archive, Venice, Calif.—courtesy Ruth Goldberg; Michael Ochs Archive, Venice, Calif.—Michael Ochs Archive, Venice, Calif.; Rex USA, New York. **143:** Michael Ochs Archive, Venice, Calif. (4)—Jane Hale/*The Flint Journal*. **144:** © Neil Zlozower, Los Angeles, Calif.—Michael Ochs Archive, Venice, Calif. (3); Westenberger/Sygma, New York. **145:** Bob Gruen/Star File, New York; Michael Ochs Archive, Venice, Calif. (5); Gary Gershoff/Retna Ltd., New York. **146, 147:** Charlyn Zlotnik/Michael Ochs Archive, Venice, Calif.—Janet Macoska/Michael Ochs Archive, Venice, Calif.; David Corio/Michael Ochs Archive, Venice, Calif. **148:** David Redfern/Retna Ltd., New York. **149:** Peter Figen/Retna Ltd., New York—Ken Regan/Camera 5, New York—Robert Blakeman, Los Angeles, Calif. **150:** Brian Lanker, Eugene, Oreg. **151:** Jay Dickman. **152:** Ken Regan/Camera 5, New York—Michael Benabib/Retna Ltd., New York. **153:** M. McInnis/Star File, New York. **154, 155:** Globe Photos, New York; courtesy CNN, Atlanta, Ga. **156:** Corbis/Bettmann. **157:** Movie Still Archives, Harrison, Nebr.; Everett Collection, New York. **158:** Alan D. Levenson/*Time* Magazine—Everett Collection, New York; Photofest, New York—The Simpsons™ and © 1990 Twentieth Century Fox Film Corporation. All rights reserved. **159:** Frank Carroll/NBC/Globe Photos, New York. **160:** NBC/Globe Photos, New York; CBS Photo Archives, New York—CBS Photo Archives, New York; Everett Collection, New York—Photofest, New York. **161:** NBC/Globe Photos, New York. **162:** Scull/Globe Photos, New York—Photofest, New York—Christopher Little/Outline Press, New York. **163:** George Lange/Outline Press, New York (2)—AP/Wide World Photos. **164, 165:** Universal/courtesy The Kobal Collection, New York; private collection. **166:** Photofest, New York—Hershenson-Allen Archive, West Plains, Mo. **167:** © Lucasfilm Ltd., & ™. All rights reserved. Used under authorization. Courtesy of Lucasfilm Ltd. **168:** Hershenson-Allen Archive, West Plains, Mo.— Everett Collection, New York. **169:** Photofest, New York. **170:** Courtesy of Joel Finler, London. **171:** The Kobal Collection, New York. **172:** Andy Schwartz—Universal/The Kobal Collection, New York—Photofest, New York—The Kobal Collection, New York. **173:** Paul Jasmin/Visages, Los Angeles, Calif. **174:** Everett Collection, New York. **175:** No credit. **176, 177:** Hershenson-Allen Archive, West Plains, Mo. © The Estate of Keith Haring. **179:** © The Estate of Keith Haring; Paschall/Taylor, courtesy Michael Graves, Architect, Princeton, N.J.—Mary Boone Gallery. **180:** Private collection. **181:** A. Tarsches/Liaison Agency, New York— private collection. **182:** Hershenson-Allen Archive, West Plains, Mo. **183:** Photofest, New York—© Peter Cunningham, New York. **184:** Clive Barda/Performing Arts Library, London. **185:** Greg Heisler, New York.

BIBLIOGRAPHY

BOOKS

Abrams, Herbert L. *"The President Has Been Shot."* New York: W. W. Norton, 1992.

America A to Z. Pleasantville, N.Y.: Reader's Digest, 1997.

American Decades: 1980-1989. Ed. by Victor Bondi. Detroit: Gale Research, 1996.

Ashe, Arthur R., Jr. *A Hard Road to Glory—Boxing: The African-American Athlete in Boxing.* New York: Amistad, 1993.

Barnard, Stephen. *Rock: An Illustrated History.* New York: Schirmer Books, 1986.

The Baseball Encyclopedia. New York: Macmillan, 1984.

The Best of Sports Illustrated. New York: Sports Illustrated, 1996.

Brode, Douglas. *The Films of Steven Spielberg.* New York: Carol Publishing Group, 1995.

Brooks, Tim, and Earle Marsh. *The Complete Directory to Prime Time Network TV Shows: 1946-Present.* New York: Ballantine Books, 1979.

Bufwack, Mary A., and Robert K. Oermann. *Finding Her Voice: The Saga of Women in Country Music.* New York: Crown Publishers, 1993.

Burrough, Bryan, and John Helyar. *Barbarians at the Gate.* New York: Harper & Row, 1990.

Cannon, Lou. *President Reagan: The Role of a Lifetime.* New York: Simon & Schuster, 1991.

Castleman, Harry, and Walter J. Podrazik. *Watching TV.* New York: McGraw-Hill, 1982.

Champlin, Charles. *George Lucas: The Creative Impulse: Lucasfilm's First Twenty-Five Years.* New York: Harry N. Abrams, 1997.

Chiu, Tony. *CBS: The First 50 Years.* Los Angeles: General Publishing Group, 1998.

Chronicle of America. New York: DK Publishing, 1997.

Chronicle of the Cinema. London: Dorling Kindersley, 1995.

Chronicle of the Olympics: 1896-1996. New York: DK Publishing, 1996.

Chronicle of the 20th Century. London: Dorling Kindersley, 1995.

Collins, Bud (ed.). *Bud Collins' Modern Encyclopedia of Tennis.* Detroit: Visible Ink Press, 1994.

Country: The Music and the Musicians. New York: Abbeville Press, 1994.

Crothers, Tim. *Greatest Teams.* New York: Bishop Books, 1998.

Curran, James W. "The CDC and the Investigation of the Epidemiology of AIDS." In *AIDS and the Public Debate.* Amsterdam: IOS Press, 1995.

Davidson, James West. *Nation of Nations.* New York: McGraw-Hill, 1994.

Denis, Christopher Paul, and Michael Denis. *Favorite Families of TV.* New York: Citadel Press, 1992.

D'Souza, Dinesh. *Falwell.* Chicago: Regnery Gateway, 1984.

Encyclopedia of the American Presidency (Vols. 2 and 3). Ed. by Leonard W. Levy and Louis Fisher. New York: Simon & Schuster, 1994.

Fawcett, Anthony. *John Lennon: One Day at a Time.* New York: Grove Press, 1976.

Fineberg, Jonathan David. *Art Since 1940.* New York: Harry N. Abrams, 1995.

Goldberg, Robert, and Gerald Jay Goldberg. *Citizen Turner.* N.p., 1995.

Gretzky, Wayne. *Gretzky: An Autobiography.* New York: HarperCollins, 1990.

Groening, Matt. *The Simpsons.* New York: HarperPerennial, 1997.

Hassan, John, ed. *The 1997 Information Please® Sports Almanac.* Boston: Houghton Mifflin, 1996.

Henderson, Rickey. *Off Base.* New York: HarperCollins, 1992.

Herbert, Solomon J., and George H. Hill. *Bill Cosby.* New York: Chelsea House Publishers, 1992.

Hersch, Hank. *Greatest Football Games of All Time.* New York: Bishop Books, 1997.

Hickok, Ralph. *A Who's Who of Sports Champions.* Boston: Houghton Mifflin, 1995.

Hilliard, Robert L., and Michael C. Keith. *The Broadcast Century.* Newton, Mass.: Butterworth-Heinemann, 1997.

The Illustrated History of Country Music. New York: Random House, 1995.

Jackson, Michael. *Moonwalk.* New York: Doubleday, 1988.

Jennings, Peter. *The Century.* New York: Doubleday, 1998.

Jesse Jackson. Ed. by Robert Jakoubek. New York: Chelsea House Publishers, 1991.

Johnson, William Oscar. *The Olympics.* New York: Bishop Books, 1992.

Kavanagh, Jack, and James Tackach. *Great Athletes of the 20th Century.* New York: Gallery Books, 1989.

Kent, Zachary. *Ronald Reagan* (Encyclopedia of Presidents series). Chicago: Childrens Press, 1989.

Kerrod, Robin. *The Illustrated History of NASA.* London: Prion, 1986.

Kingsbury, Paul. *The Grand Ole Opry.* New York: Villard Books, 1995.

Koop, C. Everett. "The Early Days of AIDS As I Remember Them." In *AIDS and the Public Debate.* Amsterdam: IOS Press, 1995.

Levy, Peter B. *Encyclopedia of the Reagan-Bush Years.* Westport, Conn.: Greenwood Press, 1996.

Lipofsky, Steve. *Bird.* Lenexa, Kans.: Addax Publishing, 1998.

McDonough, Will, et al. *75 Seasons.* Atlanta: Turner Publishing, 1994.

McNeil, Alex. *Total Television.* New York: Penguin Books, 1996.

Marschall, Rick. *The History of Television.* New York: Gallery Books, 1986.

Morton, Andrew. *Diana.* New York: Simon & Schuster, 1992.

Nebergall, P. J. *Hard Core.* Port Townsend, Wash.: Loompanics, 1997.

Nelson, Havelock, and Michael A. Gonzales. *Bring the Noise.* New York: Harmony Books, 1991.

Nicholson, Lois P. *Oprah Winfrey.* New York: Chelsea House Publishers, 1996.

O'Brien, Lucy. *She Bop.* New York: Penguin Books, 1995.

The Official NBA Basketball Encyclopedia. New York: Villard Books, 1994.

The 100 Greatest TV Shows of All Time. New York: Entertainment Weekly Books, 1998.

Our Glorious Century. Pleasantville, N.Y.: Reader's Digest, 1994.

Our Times. Atlanta: Turner Publishing, 1995.

Piesman, Marissa, and Marilee Hartley. *The Yuppie Handbook.* New York: Pocket Books, 1984.

Rap on Rap. New York: Delta, 1995.

Reagan, Ronald. *An American Life.* New York: Simon & Schuster, 1990.

Rolfe, John. *Nolan Ryan.* Boston: Little, Brown, 1992.

The Rolling Stone Illustrated History of Rock and Roll. Ed. by Anthony DeCurtis, James Henke, and Holly George-Warren. New York: Random House, 1992.

Sackett, Susan. *Prime-Time Hits.* New York: Billboard Books, 1993.

Schnabel, Julian. *Julian Schnabel: Paintings, 1975-1987.* Ed. by Nicholas Serota and Joanna Skipwith. London: Whitechapel Art Gallery, 1987.

Simora, Filomena (comp. and ed.):
The Bowker Annual: Library and Book Trade Almanac, 1989-90. New York: R. R. Bowker, n.d.
The Bowker Annual: Library and Book Trade Almanac, 1990-91. New York: R. R. Bowker, n.d.
The Bowker Annual of Library and Book Trade Information, 1981. New York: R. R. Bowker, n.d.

Stambler, Irwin. *Encyclopedia of Pop, Rock, and Soul.* New York: St. Martin's Press, 1989.

The Story of Rock 'n' Roll. Miami, Fla.: Carlton, 1995.

Thompson, Robert J. *Television's Second Golden Age.* New York: Continuum, 1996.

Trump, Donald J. *Trump.* New York: Random House, 1987.

The TV Guide TV Book. New York: HarperPerennial, 1992.

Walsh, Michael. *Andrew Lloyd Webber.* New York: Harry N. Abrams, 1992.

Ward, Ed, Geoffrey Stokes, and Ken Tucker. *Rock of Ages.* New York: Rolling Stone Press, 1986.

Wayne Gretzky. New York: House of Collectibles, 1996.

Whittemore, Hank. *CNN: The Inside Story.* Boston: Little, Brown, 1990.

The World Almanac and Book of Facts: 1998. Mahwah, N.J.: World Almanac Books, 1997.

PERIODICALS

Axthelm, Pete. "Martina Navratilova." *Newsweek,* Sept. 6, 1982.

Barol, Bill. Untitled article on the 1980s. *Newsweek,* Jan. 4, 1988.

Beck, Melinda. "1989 AIDS." *Newsweek,* July 3, 1989.

Bellm, Dan. "And Sew It Goes." *Mother Jones,* Jan. 1989.

Blauner, Peter. "Hard-Core Kids." *New York,* May 26, 1986.

Bloom, Steve. "The Hottest Lips in America." *Rolling Stone,* Nov. 8, 1984.

Burwell, Bryan. "Super Deals for Superstars." *Black Enterprise,* July 1984.

Davis, Francis. "A Master's Voice." *Rolling Stone,* Mar. 28, 1985.

Dowd, Ann Reilly. "What Managers Can Learn From Manager Reagan." *Fortune,* Sept. 15, 1986.

Eisenberg, Evan. "Bobby McFerrin." *Nation,* July 20/27, 1985.

Fricke, David. "Anita Baker Cooks." *Rolling Stone,* Oct. 23, 1986.

Gates, David. "Band-Shell Bop: Putting the Corn in Cornet." *Newsweek,* April 6, 1987.

Gentry, Jerry. "The NAMES Project: A Catharsis of Grief." *Christian Century,* May 24-31, 1989.

Hitchner, Earle. "Returning to His (Grass) Roots." *Wall Street Journal,* Dec. 30, 1997.

Hoerburger, Rob. "Anita Baker's Quiet Storm." *Rolling Stone,* Nov. 20, 1986.

"Icons of the '80s." *U.S. News & World Report,* Dec. 25, 1989-Jan. 1, 1990.

"Ivan Boesky Is Settling Some Debts." *Business Week,* Feb. 25, 1991.

Katz, Susan. "It's a Bird! It's a Trumpet! It's Wonder Voice!" *Newsweek,* Oct. 6, 1986.

Lacayo, Richard. "The '80s." *Life: 40 Years of Rock and Roll,* Dec. 1, 1992.

Langway, Lynn. "After the Games, the Cash." *Newsweek,* Aug. 20, 1984.

Levine, Dennis. "Hail Felons Well Met." *Newsweek,* Oct. 7, 1991.

Life, Jan. 1980-Jan. 1990.

Life: Diana, Portraits of a Lady, Nov. 1997.

Miller, Holly G. "Julio Iglesias: Wooing America." *Saturday Evening Post,* Dec. 1985.

Norment, Lynn. "Luther Vandross: The Voice That Seduces Millions." *Ebony,* Dec. 1985.

PEOPLE Weekly, Jan. 1980-Jan. 1990.

Phillips, Kevin P. "Reagan's America: A Capital Offense." *New York Times Magazine,* June 17, 1990.

Reibstein, Larry. "How Crooked Was Milken?" *Newsweek,* Oct. 22, 1990.

Rich, Frank:
"Feline Voices." *New York Times,* Oct. 7, 1982.
"Fraternite." *New York Times,* March 12, 1987.
"Mask Appeal." *New York Times,* Jan. 25, 1988.
"Real-Estate Duels." *New York Times,* Mar. 25, 1984.

Robinson, Jill. "In Search of Fitness." *Vogue,* June 1985.

"The Selling of Whitney Houston." *Newsweek,* July 13, 1987.

Sports Illustrated, Jan. 1980-Jan. 1990.

Time, Jan. 1980-Jan. 1991.

Time, Man of the Year issue (Ted Turner), Jan. 6, 1992.

West, Cornel. "The 80's: Market Culture Run Amok." *Newsweek,* Jan. 3, 1994.

"The Year of the Yuppie." *Newsweek,* Dec. 31, 1984.

OTHER SOURCES

Christopher, Maura. "Immigration to America." Available: http://www.salsem.ac.at/csacl/progs/AS_Modules/immigration.htm November 10, 1998.

"Chuck D." Available: http://www.public-enemy.com/soldiers/soldiers.html October 21, 1998.

"Emmylou Harris." Available: http://www.nashville.net/-kate/ N.d.

"Lionel Richie Awards, etc." Available: http://www.algonet.se/-erikwest/richie/bio.htm N.d.

"LL Cool J." Available: http://music.com/showcase/urban/llcoolj.html N.d.

"Luther Vandross." Available: http://www.sonymusic.com/artists/Luther-Vandross/biography.html N.d.

"Rebel Without a Pause." Song lyrics. Available: http://www.public-enemy.com/archives/lyrics/index.html N.d.

"Run DMC & the Beastie Boys circa 1984." Available: http://home.earthlink.net/-tgmoren/rundmc/bio.html N.d.

190

Time-Life Books is a division of Time Life Inc.

TIME LIFE INC.
PRESIDENT and CEO: George Artandi

TIME-LIFE BOOKS
PUBLISHER/MANAGING EDITOR: Neil Kagan
VICE PRESIDENT, MARKETING: Joseph A. Kuna
VICE PRESIDENT, NEW PRODUCT DEVELOPMENT:
Amy Golden

OUR AMERICAN CENTURY

EDITORS: Loretta Britten, Paul Mathless
DIRECTOR, NEW PRODUCT DEVELOPMENT:
Elizabeth D. Ward
DIRECTOR OF MARKETING: Pamela R. Farrell

Pride and Prosperity: The 80s
Deputy Editor: Roxie France-Nuriddin
Associate Editor/Research and Writing: Annette Scarpitta
Associate Marketing Manager: Terri Miller
Picture Associate: Anne Whittle
Senior Copyeditor: Anne Farr
Technical Art Specialist: John Drummond
Photo Coordinators: Betty H. Weatherley, Donna Garrett
Editorial Assistant: Christine Higgins

Design for **Our American Century** by Antonio Alcalá,
Studio A, Alexandria, Virginia.

Special Contributors: Michael Blumenthal, George Constable
(writing and editing); Ronald H. Bailey, Janet Cave, George
Daniels, Mimi Harrison, Jim Hicks, John Newton, Ellen
Phillips, Karen Sweet (writing); Ruth Goldberg, Jessica L. Jacob,
Daniel Kulpinski, Jane Martin, Terrell Smith, Marilyn Terrell,
Elizabeth Thompson (research and writing); Lee Hassig,
Stephen G. Hyslop, Alison Kahn, Robert Speziale (editing);
Richard Friend, Marti Davila (design); Susan Nedrow (index).

Correspondents: Christine Hinze (London), Christina
Lieberman (New York), Maria Vincenza Aloisi (Paris).

Director of Finance: Christopher Hearing
Directors of Book Production: Marjann Caldwell, Patricia Pascale
Director of Publishing Technology: Betsi McGrath
Director of Photography and Research: John Conrad Weiser
Director of Editorial Administration: Barbara Levitt
Manager, Technical Services: Anne Topp
Senior Production Manager: Ken Sabol
Production Manager: Virginia Reardon
Quality Assurance Manager: James King
Chief Librarian: Louise D. Forstall

EDITORIAL CONSULTANT
Richard B. Stolley is currently senior editorial adviser at Time
Inc. After 19 years at *Life* magazine as a reporter, bureau chief,
and assistant managing editor, he became the first managing
editor of *People* magazine, a position he held with great success
for eight years. He then returned to *Life* magazine as managing
editor and later served as editorial director for all Time Inc.
magazines. In 1997 Stolley received the Henry Johnson Fisher
Award for Lifetime Achievement, the magazine industry's
highest honor.

Other History Publications:

What Life Was Like
The American Story
Voices of the Civil War
The American Indians
Lost Civilizations
Mysteries of the Unknown
Time Frame
The Civil War
Cultural Atlas

Library of Congress Cataloging-in Publication Data
Pride and prosperity: the 80s / by the editors of Time-Life
Books.
p. cm.— (Our American century)
Includes bibliographical references (p.   ) and index.
ISBN 0-7835-5510-5
1. United States—History—1969-   2. Nineteen eighties.
3. United States—History—1969- —Pictorial works.
4. Nineteen eighties—Pictorial works.
I. Time-Life Books.   II. Series.
E876.P745 1999
973.927—dc21   98-51346
                                                  CIP

For information on and a full description of any of the
Time-Life Books series listed above,
please call 1-800-621-7026
or write:

Reader Information
Time-Life Customer Service
P.O. Box C-32068
Richmond, Virginia 23261-2068